Mill 635, Rafael Freyre - 2ft 6in gauge

Rafael Freyre is, by consensus, the 'best' mill in Cuba; best for scenery, best for locomotives, best for smoke-effects and best for kindly and obliging folk. Unfortunately, there is a down side too because it is also one of the most difficult mills to appreciate fully for a number of reasons. It is more than two hundred miles away from the next nearest major steam centre (Ciego de Ávila), diesels haul some trains, outward journeys with empties are worked tender-first and some trains operate after dark. Also, there are no hard-surface roads leading out into the fields which means that 'roads' are just dirt, so after rain, passage by car through the resultant mud is often impossible for days on end.

Perhaps due to the location of Rafael Freyre in the far east of the island, harvesting often starts later there than at those mills to its west and many an early-season visitor has been disappointed to find no activity at Rafael Freyre after having made the long trek to oriental Cuba for the express purpose of visiting this mill. The 2000 season started earlier but was plagued by locomotive failures caused apparently by difficulties with spares. Despite all this, with a little care and thought it was usually possible to make the visit worthwhile.

Alone amongst Cuban sugar mills, Rafael Freyre has a locomotive which

seemingly is kept exclusively for use on enthusiasts' specials and what a little gem it is too! Brought back into service in the mid '90s, it is thought to have been there as long as the mill has been and it still sports the No. 1 on its smokebox door despite its official number being 1180.

Now named LA MAMBISITA, this charming and diminutive 0-6-0 was built by Baldwin in 1882 with the Works No. 6456. It is, like almost all other steam locomotives in Cuba, an oil-burner and it is illustrated in idyllic surroundings with just about its maximum permitted load. At the time, it was working on the short branch north from the mill to the coastal town of Puerto Vita where it ran exclusively for an English group of enthusiasts on Tuesday 25th March, 1997.

Even if such a lovely little locomotive should not be available, a word with the *jefe* (chief) is usually all that is required to organise a special train using one of the mill's regular 2-8-0s (see pp 18-21 and page 23), always assuming that they haven't all broken down, of course! The *jefe* will not normally be too far away from the *trafico* (traffic office) and like so many of his compatriots, seems to have a soft spot for visitors which is very much appreciated by all.

1

Parque Lenin (Lenin Park) Railway - 3ft 0in gauge

During the time of the Cuban/Russian 'alliance', much construction work on the island was 'sponsored' by the Soviet Union to demonstrate the friendship which existed then between the two nations. As its name implies, one such example is Lenin Park. Situated on the southern outskirts of Havana, this large recreational area has an extensive children's playground as its main feature with a lake, tropical trees, flowering shrubs, an equestrian centre and vast grassy areas making up the rest of the space. There is also a steam-operated narrow gauge pleasure railway which runs (mainly) round the park's perimeter.

It may not be immediately obvious why such a railway should qualify for inclusion in a book dealing with sugar lines. However, the locomotives in use were once sugar mill locomotives which undergo major repairs at a suitable sugar mill when required and conversely, Augusto César Sandino's No. 1210 (Baldwin 2-6-0 of 1913) was once Lenin Park's No. 3. If more serious work is necessary (e.g. a general overhaul), the locomotive requiring it will probably go to A. C. Sandino (to the west of Havana) as this is the most convenient 3ft gauge mill for Lenin Park. Also, there is no reason to suppose that any of Lenin Park's locomotives will not revert to sugar mill use in an emergency.

The railway is extremely popular with Cubans of all ages and is scheduled to run every Saturday and Sunday when the trains will be seen to be full to overflowing. Only one steam locomotive at a time is needed to maintain the service and those not in use should be found on shed in the Park.

On Sunday 7th March, 1997, No. 1 was the locomotive in use and just in case there should be any doubt about where it was working, the location had recently been inscribed, not very subtly, on the tender. Built by the Vulcan Iron Works at Wilkes-Barre in 1917 with the Works No. 2761, this nice smart Mogul came from Habana Libre (a mill which closed in the mid '60s) where it ran as their No. 4. It is one of only two working sugar locomotives never to have been given a number in the All Cuba numbering scheme.

The other locomotive never to have been so numbered is Lenin Park's No. 2, shown on page 3 sitting in the Park's main station (!) at the head of its seven coach train on Sunday 15th March, 1998. Baldwin-built at their Philadelphia Works in 1923 with the Works No. 56920, this not-quite-so-smart 2-6-0 was originally a Manuel

Sanguily Mill locomotive from Pinar del Río Province and underwent its most recent overhaul at Augusto César Sandino Mill during 1996. It was returned to Lenin Park in time to be admired by visitors who came to Cuba for the 1997 *zafra* (sugar harvest).

Three other locomotives in various states of repair or disrepair are in the Park, but only one of these is ever likely to be used on the railway. This is another No. 3 and is a Baldwin 2-8-0 of 1920. Its Works No. is 54234, it had the MINAZ No. 1457 and came here all the way from Frank País Mill in Holguín Province (MINAZ is the Cuban Sugar Ministry). Some remains of 2-6-0 No. 36 were to be seen near the shed in 2000 and yet another No. 3, this time a 2ft 6in gauge locomotive, is preserved under cover at the half-way station. Just why a locomotive of this gauge should be on show adjacent to a 3ft gauge line is unclear, but this charming little 2-6-0 is quite a beauty and well worth visiting the Park for in its own right as it is a Porter of 1915 (Works No. 5727). It came from Gregorio Arlee Mañalich Mill (see page 8) and was allocated the running number 1108.

Visitors are attracted to the Park for many reasons and not just because of the railway. Much baseball happens here and the central car park is a popular place for Cubans to show off their vintage cars. On one visit, the author parked his modern Japanese hire car beside an English Ford Zephyr whose owners seemed quite taken aback when they discovered that their neighbours that afternoon were the same nationality as their beautifully maintained vehicle.

Tourists always stand out from the locals of course. On another occasion the author was wandering aimlessly about the Park just soaking up the atmosphere because a fuel shortage had caused the trains not to run, when he was 'accosted' by a very serious-looking gentleman who opened with the usual expression, "Where are you from?" in very good 'American' English. After the normal pleasantries had been dispensed with, he produced the book he had just been reading and enquired if it was familiar. Imagine the surprise when this turned out to be an English language edition of George Orwell's *Animal Farm*! When he was asked whether he was like those animals which were all equal or those that were more equal than the others, a sort of glazed expression came over his face and he seemed not to understand the question. It is definitely best to avoid politics at all costs whilst talking with Cubans!

Mill 107, Pablo de la Torriente Brau - Standard Gauge

When it comes to thoughts of the most spectacular workings by the steam locomotives in Cuba, one or two locations spring to mind automatically. The Altuna bank at Rafael Freyre should be one, of course (see pp 18/19), the climb up to Boris Luis Santa Coloma (The Mill on the Hill) from either direction might be another (Vol. 1, page 11) ... and the final push up to the mill at Pablo would almost definitely be a third. There are others, but Pablo is different from the first two because this last half mile or so of hard 'thrash' is in the middle of the road up a fairly narrow gap between workers' houses and the comparatively confined space makes the trains' passage all the more melodramatic.

There are some severe curves on this system and thus all the working loco- motives are Moguls with the short, fixed wheel-base that this arrangement implies, compared with Cuba's most numerous type, the 2-8-0. Two 2-6-0s are shown above in the mill yard on Friday 29th March, 1996 with No. 1703 (left) taking a well-deserved rest after bringing up a heavy train from the far *acopio* (loading point) at San Ignacio.

This particular locomotive is a rare (for Cuba) Henschel of 1920 and has the Works No. 18029. The 1996 season was one of its earliest at Pablo. Previously it had been at the nearby José Martí Mill for many years and only left when that mill had no further use for steam. Another of its redundant 2-6-0s, Alco No. 1401, is also at Pablo and José Martí's unwanted 2-8-0s have gone to two mills in La Habana Province: Rubén Martínez Villena (two) and Boris Luis Santa Coloma (one).

No. 1103 on the other hand is a long-standing member of Pablo's locomotive fleet and before being allocated its present number in the MINAZ All Cuba numbering scheme, it was that mill's No. 5. It is one of the smallest tender engines in Cuba and as such is used more often than not on yard shunting duties as shown here. It is a Baldwin locomotive of 1920 (Works No. 54052) and does see main line work on occasion, although naturally loads will be limited compared with its bigger brothers.

In the previous volume, an example of R. M. Villena's incredible stud of shunting locomotives was illustrated on page 8 where details of the 1878-built 0-4-2T were also given and three more shunters are shown here in this volume. The shunter shown on the right was photographed on Wednesday 11th March, 1998 and the others are shown on pages 6 and 10.

No. 1112 (or No. 4 if you go by the old mill-number on the smokebox door) is the oldest working locomotive in Cuba and one of only two or three coal-burners left on the coal-less island, but actually seeing it at all cannot be taken for granted. Without a permit (and sometimes even with one!) the chances are that it will remain at the back of the mill's running-shed and tantalisingly out of sight to visitors who stand a good chance of having entry through the heavily-guarded gate to the shed refused. Staff here can be particularly perverse sometimes.

The accompanying photograph was the eventual result of three separate visits to the mill during the 1998 *zafra* which involved pleading, cajoling and attempted bribery, all three of which were necessary to achieve the desired result. It was well known that the mill *jefe* would, if spoken to nicely, arrange for No. 1112, dead, to be towed out of the shed and into the open for photographic purposes, but getting it steamed was a very different proposition.

The author was a member of an organised group from England with a shed permit for R. M. Villena in 1998 and duly turned up on the correct day. Nevertheless, the 'lady' guard on the gate refused point blank to let any of the group into the shed area until the personal intervention of the *jefe*, with whom the group, fortunately, had established a friendly rapport earlier, secured admission.

No. 1112 was duly photographed in the semi-darkness of the shed interior and a suggestion was then made to him that perhaps it might be possible to have the little wonder steamed the following afternoon. The group would certainly 'see him all right' if he would, he was told. *"Si"*, said the *jefe*, *"no problemo"* and the group duly returned next day, only to be greeted by the locomotive out of the shed, but still dead as a dodo. "We will steam it for you now if you can wait a couple of hours", they said (or the Spanish equivalent), but this just was not possible due to other pre-booked commitments. The group was making a slow and sorry departure when an elderly Cuban gentleman introduced himself as the 'keeper' of No. 1112 and said that he would personally guarantee to have it steamed for us if we would care to come back again another day.

The only day available then was the day when most members of the group were due to fly back to England and not all were prepared to make a third visit to the mill on the word of an unknown octogenarian. However, those who did were not disappointed that time. No. 1112 was out of the shed, in steam and almost ready to work when they arrived, although a certain amount of tinkering by their venerable friend was necessary before the locomotive was deemed to be ready for service.

The accompanying photograph shows him doing something mysterious to the innards, and a few moments later the ancient driver and the even more ancient locomotive were running up and down past the mill buildings accompanied by much clicking of camera shutters and much whirring of camcorders. At the end of the show it was the antediluvian driver who was 'seen all right' as well as the *jefe*, but both definitely deserved their rewards as the number of times this particular locomotive is steamed in any one season must be very few indeed.

Mill 211, Rubén Martínez Villena - Standard Gauge

The dominant architectural feature of R. M. Villena is the wonderful old colonial-style office-block situated in front of the mill-buildings. It certainly dominates the photograph on page 10, but on this page it is another example from the fascinating fleet of small shunting locomotives allocated there which takes pride of place.

The chunky and powerful-looking 0-4-2ST No. 1201 was built by the Vulcan Iron Works in 1916 with the Works No. 2578 and was originally a Gregorio Arlee Mañalich locomotive where it ran for some time as that mill's No. 1. It was photographed during preparation for more shunting duties around R. M. Villena's mill and yard on Sunday 31st March, 1996, but on that occasion it was coupled with its smokebox to its train, a configuration which does not lend itself to much meaningful photography.

Working saddle-tanks are far from a common sight on Cuba's sugar railways. In fact only five are known to have been at work during the 1990s and up to the year 2000.

Those not illustrated on the pages of this volume appeared in Vol. One. In the earlier work, the odd-looking saddle-tank/pannier-tank at Carlos Manuel de Céspedes (out of use now for some years) is on page 46, two of Marcelo Salado's trio are shown on page 31 whilst the third appears in this volume on page 15. By contrast, about a dozen side-tanks have worked on the island during the same period but, for some reason best known to the Cubans, less than half that number of saddle-tanks have graced their lines. One can only wonder why the former have found proportionally so much favour compared with the latter.

As often seems to be the case in Cuba, time was pressing during the visit depicted on this page and a comparatively short stay was all that could be managed. This was most unfortunate because the author had been invited up onto the footplate of No. 1201 where there is no doubt that his lack of driving skill would have been put to the test once more. The locomotive crews there are generally as friendly and obliging as the guards around the shed area are not.

Mill 321, Julio Reyes Cairo - Standard Gauge

Just as Rubén Martínez Villena Mill is renowned for its fleet of small shunting locomotives, so to a lesser extent was Julio Reyes Cairo, until comparatively recently. There are only two there (as opposed to five at R. M. Villena) and although neither of them has seen much use during the late 1990s and the year 2000, each is particularly interesting in its own right. Henschel 2-4-0T No. 1124 of 1913 was illustrated on page 23 of Vol. One, so now it is the turn of its German cousin, No. 1123.

Built by Borsig of Berlin in 1910 with the Works No. 7619, it is an 0-6-0T and seems much larger (and therefore more powerful) than No. 1124, despite being of the same 11xx classification. The Borsig once worked at Seis de Agosto Mill in Matanzas Province and is thought to be the only operable locomotive by that manufacturer in the country. The above photograph was taken on Thursday 25th March, 1993 during a lull in the shunting activities which, happily for the crew, was coinciding exactly with their lunch time.

Once a must for most enthusiasts, the mill has lost its magnetism somewhat since staff took up attempting to extract large amounts of dollars from unsuspecting foreign visitors in the early 1990s and were not very subtle about it either. Virtually worthless items were offered for sale at ridiculous prices and the situation was worsened by the fact that some gullible folk actually bought them! Consequently all following visitors were regarded as easy game by the men at Julio Reyes Cairo and since this has become common knowledge, the easiest thing to do has been to stay away. After all, there is no shortage of mills where the atmosphere is not in any way mercenary.

Steam locomotives on Cuba's sugar railways usually proudly proclaim the name of their home mill on tender or tank-sides although there are exceptions, such as José Smith Comas Mill (pp 18/19, Vol. One) which displayed the name of Cárdenas (the nearest town) on its locomotives for some years. Julio Reyes Cairo is another oddity because it too had the name of a nearby town (Jovellanos) on the tank-sides of No. 1123 at one time, but now has reverted to an abbreviated mill-name by omitting 'Cairo' from both of its shunting locomotives. Quite why this is so is difficult to explain because, on No. 1124 at least, there seems to be ample space to get all the letters in. But this is Cuba, and seeking answers to anomalies such as this is a not-very-rewarding activity.

Mill 207, Gregorio Arlee Mañalich, 2ft 6in and Standard Gauge

When enthusiasts started visiting Cuba in anything like appreciable numbers in the early '90s, some mills were very unwelcoming to visitors who had not gone to the trouble (and expense!) of acquiring official MINAZ permits. However, information soon spread through railway circles regarding which mills tolerated unauthorised photographers around their locomotive sheds and which mills did not. Gregorio Arlee Mañalich is in La Habana Province and was, at that time, a mill which most definitely did not. For that reason it is not featured at all in the earlier book as the author was reluctant to try his luck at a mill which was reported to be particularly unfriendly. But how things change!

Gradually over the years and mill by mill, hard-line officialdom has softened so that by the turn of the century only a handful of mills still refused to allow access to casual callers. Thankfully, Gregorio Arlee Mañalich, whose pre-revolution name was Mercedita, is now a mill which most definitely does welcome visitors into and around the mill yard. A violent hurricane caused serious damage to the corrugated-iron roof of the engine-shed prior to the 1998 *zafra* so permission to enter the shed itself is usually withheld for safety reasons. In 1999 it was still 'awaiting repairs' and may well continue to do so for a few years yet.

Shown above is No. 1306 (Baldwin 2-8-0 of 1912, Works No. 38802), one of G. A. Mañalich's very smart 2ft 6in gauge locomotives, as it was setting back into the mill with a

loaded train on Monday 16th March, 1998. At that time the 2-8-0 was wearing a particularly attractive dark maroon or chocolate brown livery, depending on the eyesight of the viewer. The lettering and lining-out were in yellow, as were embellishments such as the winged-horse 'Pegasus' shown on the smokebox door, cylinder-cover and upper cabside. Works plates had received the same careful attention ... dark maroon/brown background and yellow lettering.

In 1999, early visitors to the mill were astounded to discover that instead of the tasteful and sober colour that had been on the locomotives the previous year, they were now duck-egg blue and presented quite an eye-catching spectacle, although on closer inspection not all of all of the locomotives had been repainted. As an example, the cylinder-covers of No. 1306 were still the chocolate brown/dark maroon colour of the previous year and still sported 'Pegasus' on them in yellow. This really was an odd sight and it continued on into 2000.

We saw at Julio Reyes Cairo Mill (page 7) how the full name was not featured on the side of the locomotive and here is another example of the same thing. The words 'Gregorio Arlee' have been replaced by the letters CAI which stand for *Complejo Agro Industrial,* and G. A. Mañalich is not at all alone in displaying this logo. The Cuban word for sugar mill is *central,* but it is quite usual to see the letters CAI in front of a mill name these days instead of *central.*

Mill 403, Mal Tiempo - 2ft 6in gauge

Rafael Freyre may well be most enthusiasts' favourite mill, but running it a close second is quite likely to be Mal Tiempo, the mill with the roaring railway engines.

As explained in the first volume (page 24), the low frequency rumble emitted from these hard-working little narrow gauge locomotives is unique in Cuba. It can be felt through the ground before it can be heard through the air. This 'advance warning system' is much valued by waiting photographers, perhaps dozing in the sunshine at the lineside, as the shock-waves ensure that they are unlikely ever to be taken unawares there by the unexpected arrival of a train.

Much of the line is easily accessible to car-borne visitors, but one location which is most definitely not so (unless you already know how to get there or have a well-informed guide) is this bridge over the Rio Caunao. It is about a quarter of the way into the route when travelling from Potrerillo back to Mal Tiempo as No. 1321 was doing when it was photographed on Monday 24th February, 1997. Outward-bound trains sometimes (but by no means always) stop on the bridge for the locomotive to take water from a tank hidden behind the trees on the right in this view, but there is another

'river' crossing much nearer to Potrerillo and that might well be used instead.

All Mal Tiempo's locomotives are Baldwin Consolidations and No. 1321, which has seen almost continuous use throughout the 1990s, issued forth from the Philadelphia Works in 1913 with the Works No. 40224. Having had two previous homes ... Guillermo Moncada and Panchito Gómez Toro Mills ... the present No. 1321 also had two previous numbers ... No. 7 at the former of these mills and No. 1 at the latter. It had clearly undergone a repaint during the 1996/7 closed season and was proudly sporting a nice new style of lettering on the tender.

This particular photograph was the second attempt at a satisfactory result at that location on that day. The first time the train crossed the bridge, the crew were obligingly doing what they had been asked to do and were producing volumes of thick black smoke for the small group of photographers waiting. As bad luck would have it, a strong wind was blowing towards the cameras and this put most of the locomotive in deep shadow, so the crew members were asked if they would be kind enough to take the train across again, but this time with less smoke. Didn't they do well?

Mill 211, Rubén Martínez Villena - Standard Gauge

So far, three of R. M. Villena's stud of five small shunting locomotives have been featured in *'Today's Steam on the Sugar Lines of Cuba';* one in Vol. One (page 8) and two in the present volume (pp 5/6). The fourth, No.1206, is a Henschel 0-4-0T of 1920 which has been well-and-truly out of use for some years now and thus is not illustrated, but to complete the roster, here is the fifth, No. 1311. This somewhat unusual looking tank engine has seen regular use during the 1990s and is shown on this page as it was on Wednesday 12th March, 1997, lit by the low, evening sunshine, backing a loaded train of sugar cane past the magnificent office block and into the mill for processing.

One or two other mills sport imposing pre-revolution buildings within their precincts (another notable example, painted pink, is at Marta Abreu), but there is none to compare with the one shown to such good advantage on this page. Obviously in need of a certain amount of maintenance (!), it is a wonder that it is still standing, but even the lack of paint and the wires which are hanging all over it, cannot remove the echoes of its past glory. The bell which is to be seen hanging inside the left hand tower must have had some importance at one time, but to the author's knowledge, its ringing has never been reported. If the tower was once a clock tower, the clock has long gone, probably never to return, like so many other things, sadly, in modern Cuba.

A 2-6-2T by Baldwin, No. 1311 was built in 1904 (Works No. 24839) and is the biggest as well as the scruffiest of the mill's little shunters. This is by no means meant to imply that it is neither interesting nor attractive because in the eyes of the photographer it is both. It is interesting because of its strange shape and it is attractive because in its filthy state, it epitomises the very essence of steam in Cuba today. It is a real workhorse. Shiny and well-cleaned locomotives are two-a-penny on the preserved lines of the world, of course, but disgustingly grimy locomotives like No. 1311 are much more rare these days and for that reason they have their own very special appeal to a wide range of observers.

Just why so many little tank engines are congregated at R. M. Villena is something about which we can only speculate. Nos. 1112, 1206 and 1207 were always R. M. Villena locomotives, but like No. 1201 (see page 6) which came here from Gregorio Arlee Mañalich Mill, No. 1311 is also another mill's piece of discarded machinery. In this case, the mill not wishing to retain ownership of such a particularly fine example of Baldwin's building expertise was Osvaldo Sánchez (see Vol. One, pp 6/7) where at one time it carried the commonest number amongst all of Cuba's steam locomotives ... No. 1.

Mill 403, Mal Tiempo - 2ft 6in gauge

From the mill (near Cruces) to the furthest *acopio* at Potrerillo, the Mal Tiempo system stretches no more than about a dozen miles, but after Rafael Freyre, this is probably the most delightful area through which steam locomotives run in all of Cuba. There are just two other *acopios* in use on the line, one of which is at the end of a short branch and there are strategically situated turning triangles so that tender-first running is virtually non-existent. No wonder Mal Tiempo with its hard-working locomotives is such a favourite.

Never too far from a solid-surface road, the line winds its way up and down through the pleasant (though mainly undramatic) countryside of this part of the island, allowing photographers and other enthusiasts much easier access than is afforded them by the often impassable dirt-tracks at Rafael Freyre. Mal Tiempo is also in an area where there are at least half a dozen other mills regularly using steam, all of which can be reached directly by visitors using the Great Cuban Highway *(autopista)* and 'The Road to the Mills', whereas Rafael Freyre is virtually a mill on its own.

Above, Baldwin 2-8-0 No. 1322 of 1903 (Works No. 23282) is the oldest locomotive amongst a stud with just two which date from as late as 1920. Mal Tiempo, Espartaco and Pepito Tey are the only 2ft 6in gauge mills still operating with steam in the area, but there were many more at one time and No. 1322 worked at two of them before reaching its present home. It was No. 4 at Ciudad Caracas (now standard gauge only, see page 30), and was also a Guillermo Moncada locomotive before that mill dispensed with steam altogether more than a decade ago.

A bit of a hybrid in the sense that in its present condition it contains major parts (including the boiler) from at least one other locomotive, it emerged again from the Mal Tiempo shed in the late 1990s after yet another lengthy overhaul. Even if spare parts could be obtained from abroad at the present time, the American trade embargo would make this impossible, so it is common practice to 'cannibalise' locomotives which have been stopped for other reasons, e.g. cracked cylinders or damaged frames. In Cuba, virtually nothing usable is wasted.

The photograph of No. 1322 was taken on the afternoon of Wednesday 3rd April, 1996 as it passed through a farmyard about a mile from the mill with a train of full cane-wagons from the two *acopios* along the line. The farm owner was quite happy to have his property invaded by the photographer and the animals were quite impervious to their peace being invaded by the passage of the very noisy train. To the photographer, such a sight was most memorable; to the animals, such a sight was so commonplace that only one of them seems to be taking the slightest interest. But definitely all were shaking!

Mill 413, Espartaco - 2ft 6in gauge

Locomotives on shed are a very common sight in Cuba and a line-up of three of them in steam and side by side is not all that rare either (as on page 24, Vol. One, for example), but the chances of seeing three locomotives with consecutive numbers in steam and lined up in numerical order must be regarded as just that little bit special. Of course, there are not very many places in the country where this could happen, simply because there are not very many sheds that have three or more locomotives with consecutive numbers and of those that have, out-of-service locomotives make such a line-up fairly unlikely.

All those shown above (as photographed on Tuesday 25th February, 1997) are Baldwin 2-8-0s which also originally carried consecutive numbers (6, 7 and 8) and which have spent their entire working lives on the Espartaco system. On the left is No. 1327 of 1911 (Works No. 37142), in the centre is No. 1328 of 1915 (Works No. 42093) and on the right is No. 1329 of 1919 (Works No. 52573). Not visible in the darkness of the shed behind No. 1328 is No. 1326 (Baldwin 2-8-0 of 1895, Works No. 14436), so in theory it ought to have been possible to have a four-locomotive line-up with consecutive numbers, but the fact that No. 1326 is now well into its second century means that it is far from being a regular performer and on this occasion the staff could not be persuaded to fetch it out to be included in the photograph. Perhaps other visitors might be more successful.

Unlike its close neighbour Mal Tiempo which has turning triangles at both ends of the line, Espartaco does not have any so locomotives cannot turn there and thus have to travel tender-first in one direction. The long line south to San Fernando has one or two short branches running off it and is very heavily graded so it is along here that the empties are hauled out tender-first and the heavy loaded trains hauled back by a locomotive running right way round. The much shorter line to the north only serves a single *acopio* which is no more than a mile from the mill and along there empties are usually propelled. However, Cuba is a country where few things stay the same for very long and as absolutely nothing is ever etched in stone, there is no guarantee that this 'usual' method of operation will stay unchanged for ever.

Mill 443, Pepito Tey - 2ft 6in gauge

Rafael Freyre is undoubtedly dramatic; Mal Tiempo is unquestionably noisy, but the best word to describe the third of Cuba's 'Big Three' 2ft 6in gauge systems must surely be 'charming'. This word might also be used to describe the gentleman *jefe* who, when approached, has invariably given permission for the author (and group) to roam around the shed and yard at will. If not too busy, he has on occasion also taken it upon himself to ensure that wherever possible, all the visitors' requirements are met, whether they be positioning of locomotives, smoke for better photographic effect or just information on train workings. Yes, without doubt, the author would definitely put Pepito Tey near the top of his list of welcoming mills.

A case in point is well demonstrated in the accompanying photograph taken on Thursday 6th March, 1997 which ostensibly shows a moving train passing a stationary locomotive, but it is actually nothing of the sort. Our friend had told the driver of the 'moving' train to stop at this very spot to pose for photographs and the group's request for a little (but not too much) smoke as the shadow might have been somewhat troublesome, was immediately passed on to the driver with the above result.

The locomotive shown sitting beside the fuelling stage on the left is Baldwin 2-8-0 No. 1337 of 1919 (Works No. 52236) and was originally the American Trading Company's No. 9. It came to Pepito Tey from the nearby mixed-gauge Elpidio Gómez when that mill had no further use for it.

Of similar design, but built a few years earlier is No. 1357, doing its best to look busy for the cameras. Also a Baldwin, this Consolidation left the Philadelphia Works in 1909 with the No. 33553 and is the oldest locomotive on the books. Always at Pepito Tey, No. 1357 at one time carried the name ARAMAO, but now carries the feature which differentiates some of Pepito Tey's locomotives from any of the others in Cuba ... the tall and elegant style of chimney which imparts such a distinguished look to those engines which it graces. No. 1337 on the left has the shorter, more usual chimney and the alternative styles are immediately evident, as are the different headlights. The magnificent example mounted above the smokebox door of No. 1357 really puts to shame the poor specimen on No. 1337, although this in turn is itself a finer unit than that fitted to many other Baldwin narrow gauge 2-8-0s, like those on the facing page, for example.

The 'ancient' appearance of some of the narrow gauge locomotives there combined with the old colonial-style buildings which skirt the yard, help to create the charming atmosphere which was referred to earlier and is no doubt an important reason why ordinary foreign tourists (as opposed to railway enthusiasts) are often taken there by their tour guides. One cannot imagine them being anything other than totally enthralled by the Pepito Tey experience.

13

Mill 403, Mal Tiempo - 2ft 6in gauge

Double-heading of steam locomotives on Cuba's sugar lines is a very rare occurrence indeed and in fact the author has only ever witnessed it twice: both occasions were the result of derailments and both were on the Mal Tiempo system. The first was in 1993 when No. 1321 came off the rails during an outward trip with empties and damaged the brakes of its tender. After rerailing, it was 'rescued' by the locomotive (No. 1320) off the next train to pass, coupled in front and pushed back to the shed for repair. By next day it was working again as normal.

The author's second experience of double-heading took place on Wednesday 22nd March, 1995 and is illustrated above, although this is really a bit of a cheat. Again there had been a derailment, but this time it occurred in the throat of the yard whilst No. 1345 was pushing its train of loaded wagons back towards the mill. Luckily, No. 1355 had been turning on the triangle at the time (this is just out of the picture to the right) and was pressed into service to drag its unfortunate cousin back onto the tracks, but as can be seen, it is No. 1345 which seems to be putting in most of the effort to help itself. As usual in such cases there was no shortage of Cuban onlookers, most of whom thought they were in charge and were giving a continual flow of advice until, with a grand shudder,

No. 1345 slipped back onto the track accompanied by a slightly subdued cheer from all and sundry as each congratulated himself on the success of the operation.

Both locomotives illustrated are Baldwin 2-8-0s of 1920 and carry the two highest running numbers at the mill. No. 1345 has the Works No. 54011 whilst that of No. 1355 is 53864. Also, both locomotives had worked previously at other mills; the former at Rámon Balboa and the latter at Héctor Rodriguez.

Generally of similar appearance, the only locomotive at Mal Tiempo with a real distinguishing feature is No. 1345, although this difference is best appreciated by studying the photograph on page 24 in the previous volume. A small variation in the size and height of the domes is quite apparent in the photograph above, but it is the chimney of No. 1345 which makes this engine stand out so much from its fellows. All the others have the usual parallel-sided variety, but No. 1345's is much shorter and, with its double lip, more ornate, giving this particular locomotive what can best be described as a right regal appearance. It was most unfortunate therefore, that it was this machine which decided to disgrace itself by derailing so publicly.

Mill 428, Marcelo Salado - Standard Gauge

As mentioned in Vol. One (pp 30/31) and in this volume on page 6, Marcelo Salado is the mill with the working saddle-tanks ... three of them in fact; all with different wheel-arrangements and all by different manufacturers. However, it is not often, if at all, that the three will be found working simultaneously and although it is usual for the mill to utilise just a single shunting locomotive at any one time, it is not all that uncommon for visitors to find two in use. The Davenport and Alco were illustrated on page 31 of the first volume whilst the third, No. 1343, is a 2-6-2ST Baldwin with the Works No. 24614 and is shown above as it shunted loaded wagons in the mill yard on Friday 5th March, 1999. Built in 1904, it is the oldest of the trio and also the largest.

No. 1343 is a much-travelled locomotive and one which not only has had at least two previous homes, but also one which has had a previous MINAZ number as well. Before coming to Marcelo Salado it was at George Washington and before that at Héctor Rodriguez where it ran with the number 1160, but 11xx locomotives are those with the lowest power rating and the present No. 1343 is obviously not in that category. Renumbering upwards has corrected a clear anomaly. At an earlier stage in its life the locomotive was at Manuel Martínez Prieto Mill in La Habana Province where it ran with the No. 2 and the name SILVIA.

The 'wig-wam' emblem shown on the side of the bunker (and on the cylinder-cover) is the insignia of MINAZ, the Cuban Sugar Ministry, and is in evidence more at some mills than at others. Like liveries, the display (or not) of the 'wig-wam' seems to be down to individual mills and even at those where it can be seen, it may very well not appear on all the locomotives. Marcelo Salado's two smaller shunting engines do not display it at all (this may be due to lack of space, of course), whilst the beautiful 4-6-0 No. 1342 (see Vol. One, page 30) has had it on its tender during most of the 1990s. On No. 1549 (see page 34, this volume), the wig-wam is just on the cylinder-cover.

Another very noticeable difference between each of Marcelo Salado's locomotives is the style of the lettering and of the cabside numbers. No two seem to be exactly the same, although this mill is not at all alone in displaying different styles. Very often, locomotives which have not had a great deal of work done on them during the closed season, nevertheless appear at the next *zafra* with all-new decorations, so staff will have been kept occupied for at least some of this time and will not have had just one long *siesta* from Easter to the next Christmas.

Mill 448, Simón Bolivar - 2ft 3½in gauge

One of the most disgustingly filthy mill sheds underfoot is Simón Bolivar, but it is also one of the most friendly. The *jefe* even keeps a collection of British locomotives' photographs on display in his office! Joined to nearby Obdulio Morales (see page 26) by unique (for Cuba) narrow gauge rails, its locomotives work whether the mill is working or not. For most of the last ten years Simón Bolivar has not worked, although 1996 was an exception (see page 41 in the first volume), as was 2000, when both mills worked. So, even if there is no tell-tale plume of smoke issuing upwards from the mill chimney, it is always worthwhile heading for the shed where a warm welcome awaits one along with almost ankle-deep, evil, black oil on the ground, which makes the wearing of oil-proof footwear a definite advantage.

The two locomotives featured on this page were photographed just outside the shed on Thursday 17th March, 1994 while No. 1367, on the left, was being readied for work. No. 1362, on the right, was dead and resolutely stayed so during every visit the author made during the 1990s.

No. 1367 is a Baldwin 2-8-0 of 1924 (Works No. 57792) and came to Simón Bolivar from the mixed gauge Noel Fernández Mill in Camagüey Province. There it was numbered 17 and ran on that mill's 2ft 6in gauge rails thus necessitating regauging before it was able to be of any use at its new home. Also a regauge is No. 1362, the mill's only non-Baldwin locomotive. The Vulcan Iron Works built this 2-8-0 at Wilkes-Barre in 1919 and gave it the Works No. 2984.

The tender of No. 1367 seems to be in dire need of a rub down and repaint in view of the jumble of lettering on it, but what is there gives us a bit of a clue to a piece of its past history. The word 'Morales' is just about discernible at the top, as are the figures '63' at the bottom, so it looks as though it might have been attached to No. 1363 at some time or other as that locomotive is the only one of either Simón Bolivar's or Obdulio Morales' allocation which ends in 63. Both 'funny gauge' mills have dumped locomotives and tenders in their yards and an inspection of them would no doubt throw up their origins, but tender-chasing has never been very high on the author's list of priorities (!) so confirmation (or otherwise) must wait for another visit.

Mill 435, Hermanos Ameijeiras - 3ft 0in gauge

Only two mills in Cuba had any steam operations on 3ft gauge tracks during most of the 1990s and the other, Augusto César Sandino, is featured on pages 22 and 27. 3ft gauge steam can also be seen working round Lenin Park in Havana, of course (see pp 2/3) and although ex-sugar mill locomotives work there, it is just a pleasure railway and thus obviously not a mill operation.

Hermanos Ameijeiros' locomotives did not appear in the first volume because steam has not been used all that much there during the latter half of the 1990s so, to compensate for this omission, two examples are shown in this volume; above and on p 25. San José was the pre-revolution name of Hermanos Ameijeiras which is situated in Villa Clara Province and many enthusiasts visiting the area tend to concentrate on other mills nearby where there is a better chance to see steam in use.

About a mile up the line from the mill there is an *acopio* and although the railway continues on past it, it is a loading point past which the steam locomotives rarely seem to venture. This short run with the tender-first outward trip, plus the not-very-welcoming

jefe and the fact that diesels often work there, all combine to keep many visitors away, despite the comparative rarity of the gauge in Cuba.

The photograph above shows No. 1373 at rest in the mill yard just after it had brought in a loaded train from the first *acopio* as the sun was setting on the tranquil scene. A Baldwin-built 2-8-0 of 1925 (Works No. 58755), the locomotive came to Hermanos Ameijeiras from Argelia Libre Mill in Las Tunas Province prior to 1977 and was given its present number after previously running as the somewhat optimistically numbered 1668.

The large letter 'E' in front of the cab-side number is an abbreviation of the Spanish word *Estrecha*, meaning narrow gauge, and is often to be seen on Cuban steam locomotives. Mal Tiempo Mill favours the use of this designation (see pp 9 and 11), as does Augusto César Sandino (pp 22 and 27), but it is to be seen hardly anywhere else, unless closed season painting prompts further exposure.

Mill 635, Rafael Freyre - 2ft 6in gauge

Due to the self-imposed (but somewhat restrictive) format employed in Vol. One, it was possible only to include there a single view of what most visitors regard as Cuba's most attractive mill, so now this imbalance has been addressed with the selection of views of the system's working trains which starts on this page and ends on page 23. The illustration on page 1 shows a steam-hauled special trundling along the Puerto Vita branch and one of the locomotives plinthed in the area is on page 25, so hopefully it will be felt that overall, justice has now been done to the jewel in Cuba's crown.

The photographs on this and the page opposite were taken from the same spot but on different occasions and show two of Rafael Freyre's 2-8-0s struggling manfully up the steep incline to Altuna at a point about midway along the sixteen miles of main line between the most distant *acopio* at Uvilla and the mill. The hard working Consolidations are heading into the setting sun on their way back home with loaded trains which have been split at La Vega at the bottom of the bank and are soon to be reunited with the other half of their trains in Altuna sidings. Neither picture would have been possible ten minutes later because the sun would have gone down behind the hills, so it can be imagined how hard a few hearts were thumping amongst the small groups of photographers who were just lucky enough to be able to record these scenes. On many days, trains returning in the

evening reach Altuna too late for conventional photography.

Above, Baldwin No. 1388 (Works No. 31375) of 1907 is shown as it did its best to keep its train moving up the gradient on Monday 3rd March, 1997. As trains near the summit round about this area, speeds drop almost to walking pace and the action might possibly be chased on foot by energetic photographers. However, such activity is hardly necessary as the photograph opposite shows. Although it depicts a different train on a different occasion (Monday 31st March, 1993), it was taken from the self-same spot as the train pictured above. The locomotive shown glinting in the lovely low sunlight here is another of Rafael Freyre's seven Baldwin 2-8-0s and is No. 1386 of 1919 (Works No. 52630). It is one of a pair from that year at the mill and they are the youngest locomotives at work on the system.

In common with other mills, locomotive workings vary at Rafael Freyre on a day-to-day basis and are dependent upon a number of factors. The mill might not be in operation because it is suffering a temporary breakdown or having a washout, for example. Machinery out in the fields might also be broken down. The yard might be full of loaded wagons and be unable to take any more. Following heavy rain, it might be that none of the

lorries or tractors can make their way through the mud from where the cane is being cut to an *acopio*. If it is early in Cuba's cutting season, it might be that cane this far out in the east of the island is not yet ready for cutting. A derailment (a not uncommon occurrence, unfortunately) might be blocking a vital part of the line. Delays caused by any of the above might cause trains to run in the dark. And if none of these factors applies, it might be that all the steam locomotives are unserviceable as some unlucky visitors found during 2000. Perseverance, patience and good luck are all needed in abundance at Rafael Freyre to make the best of its many and varied photographic opportunities.

Although visitors making the long trek eastwards just to enjoy the delights of Rafael Freyre will naturally be bitterly disappointed if there is no steam action for them to witness, often there will be the opportunity to arrange a private charter, possibly employing the services of the historic little 0-6-0 illustrated on page 1. A special passenger-carrying vehicle has been constructed by the mill's thoughtful staff for the use of visitors, but it is hardly a handsome piece and looks totally out of place. As a result, many visitors just climb aboard the train's caboose and ensure that the 'tourist-truck' is left behind. That way at least, a certain amount of authenticity can be achieved out on the line.

But if the worst comes to the worst, non-steam activity may have to be considered and there are many parts of the country less suitable for tourists than round here. Guardalavaca and Don Lino are two coastal resorts where many enthusiasts stay and both offer magnificent beaches for swimming, snorkelling, sun-bathing or simply watching other holidaymakers enjoying themselves. Banes is a quite beautiful little town which is not too far away inland and it even has a preserved narrow gauge steam locomotive tastefully plinthed and surrounded by flowering shrubs in a very photogenic position (see page 25) as a further draw.

The provincial capital is the bustling city of Holguín which has much of historical interest, whilst further away on the south coast is Santiago de Cuba, one of the architectural gems of the island. Exotic birds ranging from diminutive, multi-coloured humming birds to pelicans and flocks of pink flamingos can be found in the area, as can wonderful examples of the island's flora and fauna up in the southern mountains. If all else fails, many tourists (particularly the Japanese, for some reason) regard a visit to the special observation post overlooking the American base at Guantánamo as the highlight of a visit to Cuba, so there is something else a little out of the ordinary to consider. Who knows, after any (or all) of these diversions, Rafael Freyre might be working again when 'normal' activity can be resumed.

Mill 635, Rafael Freyre - 2ft 6in gauge

Plus ça change, plus c'est la même chose, goes the old adage, and the photographs of No. 1386 on these two pages illustrate the point perfectly. The literal translation of that little bit of French is 'the more things change, the more they tend to stay the same' and a dictionary definition says that, colloquially, it means 'superficial change does not alter the subject's essential nature'. Well, that's dictionaries for you! At Rafael Freyre, changing the lettering style and adding pictures to the locomotives' tenders may very well enhance their appearance, but does not (and cannot) alter the attractiveness of these marvellous little machines. So, *plus ça change, plus c'est la même chose!*

Like all the working Consolidations here, No. 1386 was built by Baldwin. It emerged from the Philadelphia factory in 1919 and thus shares with No. 1385 the honour of being one of the two youngest engines allocated to the mill. Always a Rafael Freyre locomotive, it originally carried the name GIBARA and was numbered 11 as

shown in the accompanying table which is correct up to the 1999 *zafra*. This being Cuba, there is no guarantee that these decorative embellishments will be retained indefinitely, of course, but observers have come to terms with the unique decorations and generally would be saddened by their removal.

The pictures on these two pages show how No. 1386's appearance changed during the 1990s and the other working locomotives there enjoyed similar treatment. Above it is seen in its new-style livery as it was about to come off the Teche branch and rejoin the main line at Paraiso on Friday 6th March, 1998 whilst on the page opposite it was in its old-style livery on Wednesday 31st March, 1993 about to leave the Hondura branch for the main line at La Vega. Rafael Freyre's motive power has long been amongst the smartest turned out on the island with lined-out counter-balance weights and shiny boiler-bands and in this latest form it should certainly retain its pre-eminent position. The *jefe* is understandably proud of his charges, and so he should be.

RAFAEL FREYRE LOCOMOTIVES

Present Number	Former Number	Wheel Arr't	Maker	Date	Works No.	Name	Tender Picture+
1	1180	0-6-0	Baldwin	1882	6456	LA MAMBISITA	
3§	Unknown	2-6-0	Baldwin	1924	57797		
1385	10	2-8-0	Baldwin	1919	52380	ARROYO BLANCO*	Jet Aircraft
1386	11 (or 4)	2-8-0	Baldwin	1919	52630	GIBARA*	Camel
1387	5	2-8-0	Baldwin	1905	26416	VITA*	"Bugs Bunny" (1)
1388	6	2-8-0	Baldwin	1907	31375	JUNUCUM*	"Pegasus"
1389	7	2-8-0	Baldwin	1912	37716	YABOZON*	Dove (2)
1390	8	2-8-0	Baldwin	1912	38101	CAYAGUAN*	Turquoise Swordfish
1391	9	2-8-0	Baldwin	1914	41468	CAMAYEN*	"Granma" (3)

+ From 1997.

§ ex Paraguay Mill, now o.o.u. Sometimes inaccurately reported as No. 5.

* Not now carried.

(1) Or Bugs Bunny lookalike.

(2) Dove of Peace?

(3) Fidel Castro's yacht lookalike.

Mill 105, Augusto César Sandino - 3ft 0in gauge

As mentioned in the Introduction, A. C. Sandino is the 'Phoenix' of Cuban sugar mills in that to all intents and purposes it seemed dead and finished after the 1993 season, but it sprang back into life miraculously, in time for the 1996 *zafra*. Enthusiasts were delighted because its reopening doubled (to two!) the number of mills where 3ft gauge steam locomotives could be seen in operation, particularly as the other such mill (Hermanos Ameijeiros, featured on pp 17 and 25) was tending to use diesels more and more at the expense of steam. Hermanos Ameijeiras was even 'exporting' surplus locomotives and No. 1350, a Baldwin 2-8-0 of 1916, completed its transfer to A. C. Sandino in 1993. Subsequently it has had plenty of use at its new home and can be seen at work there in 1996 on page 3 of Vol. One.

Illustrated above is No. 1382, another Baldwin 2-8-0. This one was built in 1915 with the Works No. 42690 and came to Sandino from Roberto Ramírez Delgado Mill in Granma Province. Prior to that it worked on the Cuban Central RR as their No. 07 and is shown as it trundled back towards the mill on Saturday 8th March, 1997 with a loaded train from the *acopio* at the end of the only branch on the system. As usual it had worked out tender-first with empties, done a bit of shunting at the end of this short line

and then taken its place at the head of a rake of full wagons ready to return. This did not take place immediately however, for some reason that was not apparent and the crew was able to take advantage of the delay by resting quietly in the shade. Such occurrences are a common feature on Cuban sugar lines and it was a good thirty minutes before members of staff, suitably refreshed, were able to set off slowly downhill with their train.

Two or three locomotives are usually in steam at A. C. Sandino, and one of these might well be the only working narrow gauge Henschel in Cuba, i.e. 2-6-0 No. 1405 of 1913, but there is a very special (and very sad) reason for selecting No. 1382 instead of the German locomotive for illustration on this page. It is because the rather rough-looking Baldwin is unlikely to be used again as towards the end of February 2000 the unthinkable happened ... the boiler exploded and caused severe injury to the crew of two. By the greatest good fortune, neither was mortally wounded, for which we are all heartily thankful, but the incident must surely give some cause for concern to other footplatemen in the country, and to the many enthusiasts who derive so much pleasure from just riding on Cuban steam locomotives.

The last of Rafael Freyre's fine-looking stock of Baldwin 2-8-0s to be illustrated is, fittingly, the oldest of them, as the youngest pair (Nos. 1385/6) has already been shown (see pp 19-21 and Vol. One, back cover). This grand-daddy is No. 1387 of 1905, Works No. 26416 and was caught by the camera as it passed through the outskirts of the village of Barjay on Sunday 2nd March, 1997 with a long and heavy train of loaded wagons for the mill. Surprisingly, steam would appear to be leaking from the left-hand cylinder and, as Cuban locomotives are generally renowned for their steam-tightness, this is not a very usual sight. By the next turn of duty however, there is little doubt that the leak would have been repaired and the locomotive's efficiency returned to normal.

For such a venerable example of Cuba's working locomotive stock (this one was almost ninety five years old when photographed), its external condition is truly remarkable as there is hardly a blemish to be seen on it, from the white smokebox and chimney, past the shiny boiler-bands and on to the nice display of lettering towards the rear. Rafael Freyre is rightly renowned for the smartness of its locomotives and with 'Bugs Bunny' prominently painted on the tender, the appearance of No. 1387 is typical of the care lavished on the fleet here at the country's No. 1 mill.

When trains are working to and from the fields, it is usual to see people on the locomotives' tenders and in the photograph above, two such riders are demonstrating nonchalantly that they don't need to hang on to anything to keep their balance. 'Tender-riders' are normally part of the train crew who attend to the coupling and uncoupling of wagons at *acopios* and other duties connected with the marshalling of trains en route, but just because people are riding on a tender it does not necessarily mean that they are part of the train crew. In this photograph they are, obviously, but on other occasions and on other mill systems, some of them might be locals 'hitch-hiking' a lift, or even foreign enthusiasts taking in the delights of this novel (but not very clean!) form of travel. Normally, in Cuba, nobody is refused a ride.

No. 4 is probably the only preserved locomotive seen by most car-borne visitors to Cuba as it is on display beside the car park of a popular service area on the east-bound carriageway of the *autopista* (motorway) near Aguada de Pasajeros, just a few miles past the turning to Australia Mill. Getting a clear view of the nicely presented 0-6-0 for a photograph is not very easy though because there are usually tourist buses parked right up beside it and, worse, there are usually Japanese and other foreign tourists climbing all over it! Patience and persuasive powers may very well have to be employed before an uncluttered photograph of this fine old machine can be obtained. The one above was eventually achieved during the afternoon of Thursday 8th April, 1993.

Baldwin built the nice little 0-6-0 in 1885 and it was put in place at this prominent spot not long before the 1992 *zafra*. Careful research has established that despite the works plate incorrectly showing an 1884 construction date and a Works No. of 7472, No. 4's true Works No. is 7691. Covadonga, which appears on the tender, is the pre-revolution name of Antonio Sánchez, a standard gauge mill, so why the wrong name has been used remains to be discovered since it is well known that the last home of the locomotive was Guillermo Moncada, a mill in Cienfuegos Province.

Due to its diminutive stature, the 0-6-0 was but a lowly shunting engine during much of its working life and latterly carried the MINAZ No. 1163. Before Guillermo Moncada, No. 4 was at Pepito Tey, but originally it was an Elisha Atkins locomotive with the name INEZ and the number 3. There has always been a certain amount of interchange of locomotives between mills and it continues to the present time.

Ex Mill 406, Guillermo Moncada - 2ft 6in gauge

Here is a real case of mistaken identity for sure. There was once a Vulcan 2-8-0 locomotive with the number 1439 at Carlos Baliño, but it most definitely was not a 0-4-0ST and in any case, such a machine as the one shown here could not be classified realistically in the 14xx band because it's much too small.

Again, detectives have been at work and discovered that this beautifully restored locomotive's correct number is 1157, that it was built by the Vulcan Iron Works in 1920 and has the Works No. 3092. It started life at El Vaquerito and was latterly out of use at Antonio Finalet, so why was it plinthed outside Carlos Baliño Mill, one is bound to ask? One is also bound to admit that one just doesn't know.

At El Vaquerito, No. 1157 was originally that mill's No. 4, a number which is still showing on the smokebox door. Photographed at its new home on Sunday 29th March, 1999, the fake No. 1439 made a really pretty sight as it posed for the camera in the mid-day sun.

Mill 446, Carlos Baliño - Standard Gauge

Of all the steam locomotives in Cuba, this is the one about which least is known. It is obviously an 0-4-0 and it is a standard gauge machine, but what else can be gleaned from this photograph of 'No. 1' which was taken on Sunday 21st March, 1999? Not a great deal really, although with its 'surround-cab' it looks as if it might be a tram engine, but so far as has been discovered, there were never any tramways anywhere near George Washington Mill, so even that seems somewhat unlikely.

Almost since enthusiasts have been visiting Cuba, No. 1 had been noted rusting away near the entrance to the mill's engine shed (George Washington is in Villa Clara Province) and by 1998 the little heap of scrap metal was barely recognisable as a steam locomotive at all. But just look at it now! It is no surprise that a fence has been erected round it to protect it. Very few plinthed locomotives in Cuba are deemed to be in need of such a high level of security. Obviously It has become a very prized possession and no wonder!

Mill 449, George Washington - Standard Gauge

For many many years, a look round the back of the engine shed would have found No. 1 'preserved' there and on each successive visit it would have appeared more and more run down. Imagine the delight therefore, when on Friday 5th March, 1999 it was discovered that this historically important Mogul had not only been moved into the open at the approaches to the mill, but also that it had undergone the most thorough external renovation and was now in virtually 'as new' condition. The bulk of the paint used was black, but it had been given a white smokebox and chimney and all the lettering was yellow. This gave it a very classy appearance and was in total contrast to its previous look.

One fairly important piece of equipment was missing however, and it was obvious that it had become somewhat denuded by the removal of the Westinghouse pump from the left hand side of the boiler. As nothing of use is ever wasted in Cuba, perhaps this vital accessory was needed to replace a faulty one on a working locomotive and who can blame the Cubans for that?

Unexpectedly spotted on the way into the mill on Friday 5th March, 1999 and photographed then, No. 1's MINAZ number was 1156, but along with some other ancient stock elsewhere, it is thought never to have been applied to this fine old engine. It was built by Baldwin in 1887 with the Works No. 8956 and after importation by Zozaya & Co., it ran with the name ADELA.

Mill 435, Hermanos Ameijeiras - 3ft 0in gauge

Estación Central (Central Station), Havana - Standard Gauge

Now returned to the concourse of Havana Central Station after some twenty-five years on display in Lenin Park, 4-2-2 No. 1 LA JUNTA was amongst the first dozen steam locomotives to arrive in Cuba and it is entirely appropriate that this historic locomotive should be included here because its first duties would have been on sugar traffic (sugar to the ports, for example, and materials back to the mills) as the first railways to be built on the island were all primarily sugar railways. The 4-2-2, probably in red livery, first operated on the Matanzas Railroad and was retired round about 1900. Built by Rogers, Ketchum & Grosvenor in 1843, LA JUNTA is certainly the oldest steam locomotive in Cuba and is claimed to be the oldest in the Caribbean area.

When photographed on Friday 17th March, 1995 it was dressed overall in a tasteful dark brown livery with silver smokebox, white wheel-rims and the odd bit of black here and there, but in 1999 this had changed considerably and not for the better, it was felt. What had been brown was now dark red, or at least most of it was, because a real botch job had been done of the repainting and in many places the original brown could still be seen. This was most noticeable on the tender where a rectangle had been left untouched round the name LA JUNTA and another round the building date: Año 1843. To return it to its original livery is very commendable of course, but we must hope that it will not be too long before a proper and complete paint job is given to Cuba's most venerable steam locomotive.

The tiny EL PANCHITO from Nicaragua Mill, Holguín Province, is one of the most thoughtful and sensible examples of all Cuba's outdoor preserved locomotives as it is under a canopy to give some protection from the sun and the rain and it is beside a road near the centre of the town of Banes where it can be admired very easily by all. There is no nasty fence to look through, no impenetrable compound to peer into and no armed guard shouting "Thou shalt not pass", (in Spanish, of course) as if his very life depended upon it. In a freely accessible public place, EL PANCHITO is surrounded by palm trees and beautiful flowering shrubs so, apart from a rather inconveniently positioned safety rail, visibility could hardly be improved.

H. K. Porter built this diminutive 0-4-0 at their Locomotive Works in Pittsburgh, Pennsylvania from where it emerged in 1888 with the Works No. 964. Prominent on the side of the smokebox, level with the chimney, is the shiny, shield-shaped works plate which is made of brass, has lettering backed with red and confirms all these details. What it doesn't say (and in fact couldn't say) is that the locomotive ran with the number 1 when it was at Nicaragua, it was never allocated a MINAZ number and, early in its life, it belonged to Hippolito Dumois of Havana. Aren't we lucky that, despite all their troubles, the Cubans are still able to instigate such an active and on-going static preservation programme which is demonstrated by the six representative photographs on these two pages?

Mill 607, Nicaragua - 3ft 0in gauge

Mill 418, Obdulio Morales, 2ft 3½in gauge

As described in Vol. One, the existing lines in the Obdulio Morales/Simón Bolivar area were once part of a forty mile long, 2ft 3½in gauge public carrier railway which connected the towns of Chambas and Caibarién on the north coast of the island. This explains why such an 'odd' gauge has been perpetuated today, although it does not explain why the gauge was chosen in the first place. The reason for this has no doubt been swallowed up by the passage of time.

The two mills' railways are always worked as a single system, even though it is common practice for only one of the mills to be in operation at any one time and, during most of the 'nineties (with just one exception ... 1996), that mill has been Obdulio Morales. In 2000, surprisingly, both were working. On the occasion this photograph was taken (Tuesday 3rd March, 1998), the locomotive on the left, No. 1420, was just arriving with a loaded train from Simón Bolivar whilst the locomotive on the right, No. 1367 (see also page 16), was waiting with a caboose to shunt the train into the mill. Some diesels have invaded the system recently and it was a stroke of great good fortune that brought these two steam locomotives (one from each mill) together on that particular afternoon.

No. 1420 is the one shown operating on home ground and is a Baldwin 2-8-0 of 1920 with the Works No. 53847. Prior to the introduction of the All Cuba numbering system it was this mill's No. 6. Not always a 'funny gauge' locomotive, it was originally built to work on 3ft gauge track which it did at two previous homes; the mills of Heriberto Duquesne and Chiquitico Fabregat, both in Villa Clara Province. At the latter it was their No. 8. The much travelled machine was completely rebuilt in the mid 1990s when the frame of scrapped locomotive No. 1542 was used to replace the original one which had become unserviceable.

The locomotive on the right, No. 1367, has been traced to just one previous home and that too was not a 2ft 3½in gauge mill but the dual gauge (standard and 2ft 6in) Noel Fernández in Camagüey Province whence the smokebox number 17 originates. With only 2½in to adjust, the conversion was that much easier than it would have been from a 3ft gauge locomotive. Another Baldwin 2-8-0, No. 1367 is a Simón Bolivar locomotive that was built in 1924 and has the Works No. 57792.

Mill 105, Augusto César Sandino - 3ft 0in gauge

After the unfortunate events described on page 22, it is a pleasure to report that at the end of the 2000 *zafra*, No. 1404 (above) was still going strong and showed no signs of disgracing itself in the manner of No. 1382. Perhaps not quite as steam-tight as it might have been, it was nevertheless more than a match for its heavy train as it raced across the main road just a couple of hundred yards from the mill when it was captured on film on Thursday 12th March, 1998. No concession to road traffic here, you notice!

No. 1404 is an Alco Consolidation (the only one by that manufacturer at the mill) and was built at their Cooke Works in Paterson, New Jersey in 1919 with the No. 58746. When it first arrived in the country it was to run on a 3ft gauge branch of the Cuban Central Railroad and carried the unusual running number 018. Later it was at Frank País Mill in Holguín Province (right at the other end of the island) before it settled down, probably to end its days at A. C. Sandino as there is now almost nowhere else on the island that would have much use for it.

The lack of heavy exhaust smoke came as something of a surprise to the waiting photographers on this occasion as the loaded train had only just reached the small summit at the road-crossing before it had to drop down into the mill yard. At other times locomotives had been noted smoking profusely right up to the storage sidings. Luckily the much-reduced exhaust allows the beautiful Cuban sky to be seen to good advantage. It is not too often that such skies, full of fluffy white clouds, allow the sun to shine through at exactly the right moment to encourage successful photography of the passage of a train, which is what happened this time. As every serious railway photographer knows only too well, it is frequently just the opposite with the only small cloud in the sky hiding the sun just as the train passes. Ever cynical, enthusiasts call this the 'photographers' cloud', and many swear that it follows them around the world, but it must have got lost on this occasion and the small group which witnessed this scene was very pleased that it had.

Mill 303, Australia - Standard Gauge

As well as being one of Cuba's longest steam-operated systems, Australia also has one of Cuba's more interesting locomotive studs in that it is the only mill with two main line Henschel Moguls plus an Alco 4-6-0 and the obligatory collection of Baldwins, two of which have been converted to diesels, unfortunately. It is not unusual to find four or five locomotives in steam at any one time there, and with its steep grades and flat crossing over the *autopista*, it is no surprise that despite a rise in the mercenary tendency of some staff, Australia is one of the country's most popular mills amongst enthusiasts.

Another attraction of Australia is that there are turning facilities for the locomotives at both ends of the line which means that there is very little tender-first running. The Henschels were illustrated in Vol. One, pp 12/13, and the Alco has been constantly 'under repair' for some years now, so the locomotive chosen to represent the mill here is Baldwin 2-8-0 No. 1513 (Works No. 54067) of 1920. It was caught on Saturday 19th March, 1994 after it had just topped up at the water tank about a mile before the *autopista* during an outward journey with empties for San Ramón at the far end of the line. Sadly, recent visits to the line give the impression that this facility has been allowed

to fall into disuse.

The locomotive's past history shows a certain amount of journeying as immediately prior to arriving at Australia, it worked at Manuel Martínez Prieto Mill in La Habana Province. Before that it was at Comandante Manuel Fajardo Mill, also in La Habana Province where it ran with the number 3. It has proved to be a reliable workhorse at its latest home and has often been found in steam by visitors during the last few years.

Although not visible in this photograph, there is a water-carrying vehicle immediately behind the tender. It is normal practice to take water out to the far *acopio* with every train as there is no permanent water supply at that somewhat remote spot. There is a tall water-tank there and water is pumped up to it to keep a supply on site. The very friendly workers at that distant location have been known to ask visitors to 'have a go' working the loading machinery and many a red face has retired ignominiously from the building after making a real 'pig's ear' of the operation as it is far from being as easy as it looks.

Mill 107, Pablo de la Torriente Brau - Standard Gauge

Examples of the work of five different locomotive manufacturers are to be found at Pablo and the lowest numbered engine on the island (Vulcan Iron Works 0-6-0ST No. 1101 of 1907) is carefully preserved here under cover, although at a recent inspection it was definitely in dire need of a fresh lick of paint. The Henschel and one of the Baldwins are illustrated on page 4 and No. 1501 (the locomotive pictured on this page) was to be seen brewing up on page 4 of the first book, but to demonstrate that it did indeed work trains sometimes (even if not all that often), it is shown above soon after arrival at the end of the short line to the north of the mill as it was about to set back into the *acopio* with the empties it had just brought out.

All the steam locomotives on Pablo's books are six-coupled machines, whether they be preserved, 'under repair' or working and the only non-Mogul at the mill is the preserved 0-6-0 saddle tank mentioned above. It is quite unusual for a mill not to possess a 2-8-0 and it is almost as unusual for the whole working fleet at any mill to be of the same wheel arrangement, but at Pablo both these parameters apply.

No. 1501 was photographed on Wednesday 29th March, 1995 and at that time it was a hundred and one years old, not something that many locomotives in the world, still working regularly, could have said about them. This particular one was built by Rogers as a 2-6-2T and has the striking works number of 5000. Latterly, the venerable old machine has been out of use, but it is hoped that whatever it is that has stopped it working is not too serious and that it will not be too long before once again it is taking its rightful place at the head of Pablo's trains and thrashing up the hill between the houses, exuding wondrous sights and sounds to the delight of us all.

Mill 404, Ciudad Caracas - Standard Gauge

An irregular user of steam during the 1990s, this easily accessible mill is often given a miss by enthusiasts driving up and down 'The Road to the Mills' because they prefer the certainties (?) of steam activity at Ifraín Alfonso or Mal Tiempo say, to the uncertainties of steam at Ciudad Caracas which is in Cienfuegos Province. Nothing particularly unusual or spectacular is likely to be encountered there, but the mill does house a 2-6-2 and by timing a visit correctly, it might well be found in steam as it was on Saturday 13th March, 1999 when the above photograph was taken.

Ciudad Caracas' pre-revolution name was just Caracas (one wonders why it was thought necessary to change it!) and just like nearby Carlos Caraballo (see Vol. One, page 33), it has been in and out of use during the 1990s. The mill's Baldwin 2-8-0 No. 1724 and Alco 2-6-0 No. 1725 (both 1920-built locomotives) were employed on inter-mill workings at different times during this period, but it is the 2-6-2 which is the main draw and actually finding it at work is always regarded as a bit of a bonus.

The attractive little locomotive carries the number 1538 and is another Baldwin of 1920 (Works No. 54230). It was originally a tank engine, although just when and why it was converted to run as a tender engine is not clear. It has always been at Ciudad Caracas (it ran earlier as their No. 2) so it would appear that in all probability the modification was carried out there. Removing the side-tanks and adding a tender (there is never a shortage of tenders hanging around from redundant locomotives) would be no big deal and a modification that is well within the capability of any Cuban steam shed in this day and age.

In one respect, the operation at Ciudad Caracas is similar to that employed at many other mills in that the first *acopio* out from the mill is no more than a couple of hundred yards or so away from the mill itself and there has been much speculation regarding this seemingly wasteful arrangement. "Why not take the cane the little extra distance directly into the mill and thus avoid double-handling?", people ask. However, there are several good reasons why this is not done and one is simply that it tends to reduce congestion at the mill itself. Another is that if the mill is suffering a temporary shut-down, cane can still be brought in from the fields and stored at the *acopio,* whilst a third reason is the valuable ability to regulate cane flow into the mill throughout the day. Keeping lorries and tractors on the move during daylight hours is vitally important, whereas keeping loaded railway wagons waiting nearby until after dark ensures that the mill can keep working round the clock. So, building an *acopio* close to a mill is not as daft as it appears at first sight.

Mill 409, Antonio Sánchez - Standard Gauge

There is always something strangely romantic about seeing a train (any train) running down the middle of a town (or village) street and in Cuba there are at least three places where steam-hauled trains have done this regularly of recent years. Perhaps the best known of these is shown on page 43 of Vol. One with 4-6-0 Alco No. 1736 thrashing through Limones Palmero at the far end of the Orlando González Ramirez system, whilst another (almost as well known but not illustrated), is at Pablo de la Torriente Brau. The third is at Antonio Sánchez Mill in Cienfuegos Province and an interesting event that occurred on Saturday 28th February, 1998 is illustrated on this page.

Some of Cuba's sugar mill railway systems are extremely complex and many mills are 'joined' to each other by rail, either directly on MINAZ metals as here or via the FCC with which they have a connection. In this case the adjacent mill is Primero de Mayo (about ten miles away) and it is one of that mill's locomotives, No. 1545 (also featured on page 33) which is shown proceeding slowly up the 'High Street' at Antonio Sánchez with a long train of empties.

Just because a mill is not working does not necessarily mean that its locomotives are not needed and Primero de Mayo Mill was not working on the day this photograph was taken, but as can be seen, at least one of its locomotives was. Antonio Sánchez's locomotives were not all idle though and, earlier in the day, Baldwin 2-8-0 No. 1624 was seen shunting molasses hoppers close to the mill.

No. 1545 is a Baldwin of 1915 with the Works No. 42347 and is one of a matching pair of Moguls with consecutive running numbers and works numbers that are allocated to Primero de Mayo. The other (not illustrated) is No. 1546 (Works No. 42348) and the two of them have spent the whole of their working lives here. Both previously carried other numbers; the former's were 7 and 4 whilst the latter's were 9 and 5.

Footplate rides in Cuba are usually there just for the asking and often without asking too which sometimes makes them harder to refuse than to accept! Once up on the footplate it will probably not be long before the regulator will be entrusted to the visitor and this hands-on experience is, to the author at least, one of life's great adventures. Actually starting a train from a dead stand **without slipping** is an acquired talent, particularly as all locomotives' regulators seem to have a different feel, and few achievements make the author as happy as being able to do this, although in all truth it must be admitted that success has always been a little elusive, to say the least! In Britain, a footplate ride on a steam locomotive must follow extensive form filling-in, yellow vest-wearing and knowing whom to speak to in the first place, but in Cuba it's just turn up, climb up and prepare to get your hands dirty. Yes, footplating the locomotives is all part and parcel of the great Cuban steam scene.

But successful photography from the footplate of a moving steam locomotive is a different matter altogether and achieving a satisfactory result is even more problematical than photography from the lineside. For a start, the state of the track in Cuba is such that one is prompted to wonder most of the time how the locomotives and trains ever manage to stay on the rails. This makes it necessary to hang on for grim death, which leaves only one hand to operate the camera equipment. Touching anything on the footplate of a Cuban steam locomotive immediately covers one with thick, black oil and in no time at all, this is all over the cameras. It just can't be helped though, but obviously doesn't do them any good whatsoever.

Then there is the question of the camera settings. Too slow a shutter speed and everything will be blurred of course; a fast shutter speed leaves no depth of field and much of the scene out of focus, but it is this latter method that the author always uses on the footplate so that at least some of the photograph is sharp ... he hopes! It's no use trying to support the camera on any part of the locomotive either, because that will be bucking worse than a bronco, so it's knees bend (to absorb shocks), take a deep breath and fire off three or four exposures in the hope that at least one will be OK each time. The cost of film compared with all the other expenses involved in getting to Cuba is always at the low end, so the philosophy that if you take enough photographs, one

Henschel 2-6-0 No. 1716 at a bullock-worked *acopio* on the Australia system, Good Friday, 9th April 1993

Mill 428, Marcelo Salado - Standard Gauge

or two are bound to be reasonable, has always seemed to be the most sensible approach. Like Vol. One, all the b&w photographs in this volume were taken on Ilford FP4 Plus film with a Canon F1 35mm camera fitted with a standard (50mm) lens.

The locomotives shown in the footplate views have both been featured before: No. 1342 (left) is on page 30 of the first volume, and No. 1545 (right) has just been seen on page 31 of this book as it left Antonio Sánchez Mill for Primero de Mayo. The ride on 4-6-0 No. 1342 started half way along the roadside stretch from Remedios to Marcelo Salado when the train had stopped in order that some attention could be paid to the locomotive's running gear and ended at the far end of the mill yard when No. 1342 came off and 2-6-2ST No. 1343 (see page 15) took over to shunt the loaded wagons back into the mill. The accompanying photograph was taken at the approaches to Marcelo Salado on Friday 5th March, 1999.

The ride on 2-6-0 No. 1545 was an altogether longer trip and took place on Saturday 28th February, 1998. This was the occasion when Antonio Sánchez was processing cane from Primero de Mayo's fields and consequently, as well as its own, at least one of Primero de Mayo's locomotives was in use also. No. 1545 had brought in a loaded train earlier and, once the marshalling of empties was complete, it set off back towards home territory with the author happily ensconced on the footplate. Just short of the mill there is a triangle and, with the train occupying one side, it was used like a passing loop to allow the locomotive to run round and then propel the empties into the mill yard with its tender then coupled to the other end of the train. The photograph (right) was taken as the train approached the triangle.

The terrible accident referred to on page 22 ought by rights to deter would-be footplaters from indulging in this potentially dangerous activity, but as long as invitations continue to be extended, there is little doubt that they will continue to be accepted and, as long as the risks are appreciated (as no doubt they always are), there should be no reason why riders should not continue to enjoy this most exhilarating of all activities on Cuban railways.

A bullock-operated *chuco* (loading point) was supplying cane to Pablo de la Torriente Brau Mill in Pinar del Rio Province on Friday 29th March, 1995

Mill 424, Primero de Mayo - Standard Gauge

33

Mill 428, Marcelo Salado - Standard Gauge

It is always a satisfying experience to be able to photograph steam locomotives passing each other because it is something which is not easily planned and when it occurs naturally, photographers are almost invariably in the wrong position to make the most of it. However, on Monday 17th March, 1997, Lady Luck was smiling on Marcelo Salado. Thus the photographer was just able to get himself (more or less) into the right position as 2-8-0 No. 1426 on the left was setting back towards the shed and 2-8-0 No. 1549 was stomping in with a loaded train from somewhere the other side of Remedios. The angle of the sun could be said to be a little less than ideal, but occasions like this do not present themselves very often and should be grabbed thankfully with both hands when they do.

The big surprise on this occasion was the arrival of the two trains so quickly one after the other. About ten minutes before this photograph was taken, No. 1426 had arrived with loaded wagons and, as usual, had left them in the yard to be dealt with by the yard shunter which on that occasion was 2-6-2ST No. 1343. Whilst this was going on and the Mogul was trundling back gently towards the shed, a column of thick black smoke was suddenly spotted approaching at some speed and it was realised

somewhat belatedly that a 'passing shot' might be possible. This meant that a swift trot would have to be made to get to the right place by the right time and running in Cuba's midday heat is an activity which should never be undertaken lightly.

That the resultant photograph has turned out as sharp as it has is as big a surprise to the photographer as it must be to everyone else, because after his exertions, his hands were certainly shaking more than usual and the perspiration off his brow was partly obscuring his vision through the camera view-finder. Lady Luck doesn't put in an appearance all that often, but when she does, it is only right and proper that she is given all the credit she deserves.

No. 1426 is a Baldwin of 1920 (Works No. 53282) and No. 1549 came from the Cooke Works of Alco in 1920 with the Works No. 62620. This latter locomotive was in steam and in immaculate condition a couple of years previously when its main purpose appeared to be to allow visiting enthusiasts to drive it up and down in the yard solely for their own enjoyment. The mill was not working at the time, but it was a real pleasure to be able to 'play trains' on that occasion with the active encouragement of the staff who had been reported earlier as not always being too welcoming to foreign visitors.

Mill 107, Pablo de la Torriente Brau - Standard Gauge

Pablo is one of only three mills west of Havana that have used steam traction into the late nineties and it is by far the most spectacular. The mill at Augusto César Sandino (pp 22 and 27) is interesting because of its rare (for Cuba) 3ft gauge tracks and the fact that it was resurrected from disuse in 1996. Eduardo García Lavandero (not illustrated) has big locomotives (including, in 2000, the Porta-rebuild No. 1816, see page 40) and is a most accessible line with some roadside running, but at the height of the season at Pablo, there is the regular, incomparable 'thrash' of a 2-6-0 as it lifts its loaded train up past the houses, over a road junction and into the mill yard, an operation which can recur as often as three times an hour. The locomotive has to be a 2-6-0 because all Pablo's working locomotives are 2-6-0s.

The photograph above shows No. 1662 as it was on Wednesday 29th March, 1995 while it shunted the yard at Pablo. The locomotive was built by the Vulcan Iron Works in 1920 and its Works No. is 3081. Surprisingly perhaps, No. 1662's previous home was at Alfredo Álvarez Mill in far away Camagüey Province and before that it belonged to Escambray Mill in Sanctí Spiritus Province where it ran with the number 1. It is doubtful however, if the cab-side and tender decorations at either of these mills matched those which No. 1662 was carrying on the day it was photographed at Pablo in 1995.

In that year the lettering on some of Pablo's locomotives was striking to say the least with a bright yellow background fringed with red, and pillar-box-red letters and figures. Some observers commented that it looked as though it had been applied by a demented Picasso, but it was not to last as can be seen on page 4. The 1996 style was much more sober and, although there was a fair sprinkling of white stars here and there, the letters and numbers for that season were primrose yellow with a plain white background.

It was all change again for the 1997 *zafra* when white paint only was used and it stayed the same during 1998, but in 1999 visitors were delighted to see that once again some fancy colours (with imagination to match) had been used to brighten up the black locomotives. The decoration was not quite up to the surreal heights of 1995's 'Picasso-effect' perhaps, but nevertheless it was most attractive as a blue background had been given to red lettering with yellow borders. After so many years of drabness, it is a real pleasure to see that at last many mills are applying individual liveries and embellishments to their locomotives and it is only to be hoped that once started, this happy trend will continue.

35

Mill 522, Venezuela - Standard Gauge

The bustling little town of Ciego de Ávila is positioned both on Cuba's main east-west highway and on Cuba's main east-west railway. Access is therefore easy for the scores of enthusiasts who arrive during each *zafra* because Ciego is also at the centre of a clutch of four of Cuba's most important steam-operated mills, all within a fifteen mile radius. Ciro Redondo (see pp 42/43) is to the north, Orlando González Ramirez is west (page 44), Ecuador is south-east (page 41) and Venezuela is south (see also pp 39 and 48). Pages were devoted to each in Vol. One and are again here.

All are standard gauge mills, all have big locomotives, all have long and interesting systems and all offer great photo-opportunities both around the mill yards and out in the fields. Permits are usually required to gain access to any of their sheds, but many enthusiasts are of the opinion that the activity to be seen outside the sheds makes entry unnecessary. Anyway, there are plenty of sheds in Cuba where entry is encouraged so, as they say, if you've seen one, you've seen 'em all!

Ciego de Ávila is not in a general tourist area which means that local hotels, although adequate (just!), do not match up to those in, say, the resorts of Varadero or Guardalavaca. Some enthusiasts prefer to stay twenty miles north in the town of Morón because that gives easier access to the 'funny gauge' mills at Obdulio Morales and Simón Bolivar, but Morón's hotels are not really a lot different from those in Ciego. The trouble is, of course, that the mills around here are so attractive that they are generally a 'must' on most itineraries and if the accommodation turns out to be slightly sub-standard compared with elsewhere on the island, then so be it.

The photographs on these two pages feature just one of Venezuela's stud of nine allegedly workable steam locomotives, two of which are 4-6-0s and the remainder 2-8-0s. No. 1741 is one of the latter and is also one of a running sequence of six consecutively numbered locomotives at this mill, although they have rarely, if ever, all been noted in steam at the same time. This unusual collection is exceeded only at neighbouring Ciro Redondo which in theory has nine consecutive numbers and at Rafael Freyre which certainly has seven. However, Ciro Redondo's sequence may not truly be said to consist of workable locomotives at the present time due to that mill's policy of cannibalising some to keep others running. At least three of the nine definitely looked

permanently out of use in the late 1990s so in all probability, Venezuela's six is beaten only by Rafael Freyre's seven.

Like the majority of steam locomotives on the island, No. 1741 is a Baldwin 2-8-0; it has the Works No. 52972 and dates from 1920. Originally it belonged to the Cuba Cane Sugar Co. and was their No. 106, but since those early days it has always been a Venezuela locomotive. In 2000 it had become green!

The system there is one of Cuba's most extensive. It is not quite as far-reaching as Ciro Redondo, nor does it have as many lines, but it is a good long system nevertheless and joins up directly with one of Orlando González Ramirez's lines to the west which the author discovered to his surprise during a footplate ride in the early '90s. There is a connection with the FCC just to the north of the mill and also a connection with Ecuador to the east via the line which runs past 'The Tree' (see page 39).

The fact that Ciego de Ávila is home to a fine selection of 1950s American 'gas-guzzling' cars was referred to in the first volume and the chance to ride in one does not occur all that often, but in 1998 the author found himself in Ciego for a few days without a car, so he took the opportunity to hire a '57 Chevy (complete with driver) for a day out on the Venezuela system. The total cost was $20 (including driver and petrol) and the actual vehicle is shown posing on the left of the photograph on page 36, partly obscuring a Russian tractor which pulled up at the level crossing (in order to make the scene more interesting, perhaps?), just as the train, hauled by No. 1741, arrived. Most days in Cuba are memorable for one reason or another, but a day out chasing steam in a '57 Chevy with some Cuban friends and a chauffeur definitely ranks as one of the most memorable of the lot. The location of the photograph is near Sanguilly, the date was Thursday 2nd April and, assuredly the occasion will never be forgotten.

No. 1741 is shown again at Moreno on the same line to the west of the mill as in the previous photograph, but this time at dusk, as the glint hints. The date then was Monday 14th March, 1994 and the tree was popular with photographers at the time as it gave a satisfying frame to the scene. Unfortunately, it has not been possible to repeat this photograph of recent years because the locals, totally insensitive to the needs of visiting enthusiasts, have installed the Cuban equivalent of a not very portable Portaloo (at least that's what it looks like) under this side of the tree, thereby blocking the view. Shame, but then, that's Cuba!

Mill 405, Luis Arcos Bergnes - Standard Gauge

In 1993 No. 1755 was a George Washington locomotive and is shown on the front cover with loaded cane wagons racing an approaching thunder storm back to the mill ... a race won by the train, but only just. Then, diesels started to arrive, so George Washington decided to rid itself of some of its steam stock and No. 1755 was sent to Luis Arcos Bergnes, another mill in Villa Clara Province.

That one is north-east of Santa Clara and about five miles north of the main road to Remedios, but during most of the 1990s it was missed by many enthusiasts because the sign-post pointing to it was also missing and hills block the view of the mill chimney from the main road. L. A. Bergnes' pre-revolution name was Carmita and as well as its small but active steam fleet, it has a flat crossing with the FCC complete with small station where there is a tall semaphore signal controlled by an adjacent single lever signal box.

No. 1755 is a Baldwin Consolidation of 1917 and has the Works No. 46533. Before George Washington it was at Cándido González Mill in Camagüey Province and before

that it was the Cuba Cane Sugar Company's No. 8 at Ciro Redondo. As much-travelled locomotives go, No. 1755 is about as travelled as one can get.

For the above photograph the very smartly turned out 2-8-0 had been attached to a rake of empty wagons in the mill yard (the mill was not working at the time) and was performing a series of run-pasts on Tuesday 3rd March, 1998 for a group of (mainly) English enthusiasts, although this simple act was not without problems. The usual one of judging when the sun would come out from behind the clouds was fairly easy to overcome, but much more trouble was being caused by a field of burning stubble off to the left as the swirling wind was causing the whole site to be engulfed by thickening smoke and guessing when that would be at its lowest level really was a problem. That the locomotive is as clear as it is, is probably down more to luck than judgement, but the fact that the wagons can be seen as clearly as they are is down to a little bit of darkroom manipulation because at the time they really were very hazy indeed. Who says the camera cannot lie?

Mill 522, Venezuela - Standard Gauge

Much mention has already been made of 'The Tree', so it was thought only right and proper that it should be illustrated and this photograph shows it as it was on Saturday 25th March, 1995. Once surrounding cane has been cut, 'The Tree' is the only prominent feature in a totally barren landscape and can be seen standing out by itself from miles around. The railway does a sweeping reverse curve at this point so photography of tree and train together can be a little tricky depending on the time of day and thus the angle of the sun, but there must always be some sort of view possible, even if it has to be a going-away shot, as here. The smoke visible in front of the locomotive was coming from a large field of burning stubble off to the left as it is common practice in Cuba to clear the fields in this manner.

The locomotive is No. 1742, it has the Works No. 53853 and is another of Venezuela's Baldwin 2-8-0s of 1920 of which the mill had five (plus four others) at that time, although not all were in working condition (No. 1741 is on pp 36/37). Entry into the shed without a permit was usually denied, but not always and once inside it was possible to see that a certain amount of cannibalisation was taking place as at Ciro

Redondo in order to keep as many members of the fleet running for as long as possible. Robbing Peter to pay Paul is about the only way that the aim can be achieved in this desperately deprived country.

One thing the Cubans are not deprived of is an almost limitless amount of fertile soil and, in some parts of the island, as at Venezuela, it has a very striking orange colour. That makes it lovely to look at, of course, but if for any reason it gets inside the car it soon covers everything. Air-conditioning units as fitted to Cuban hire cars have been known to fail and thus, in the heat of the day, windows have to be lowered. Unfortunately, many of the roads giving access to the railway are dirt roads and car-borne enthusiasts hope and pray that they don't have to open any windows whilst travelling about out there. It's uncomfortable enough once this fine dust gets onto a car's occupants, but they can always wash it off at the end of the day. If it gets inside any photographic equipment the results might well be dire, so hermetically sealable bags have become a real necessity and travelling without one could lead to a total loss of photographs. Don't say you weren't warned!

Mill 428, Marcelo Salado - Standard Gauge

South Africa has its 'Red Devil' in the shape of the solitary class 26 4-8-4 locomotive No. 3450 (the Wardale-modified 25NC) and although Cuba's 'Red Devil' (No. 1816) is a much more modest 2-8-0, it is the brain-child of the great Argentinian engineer L. D. Porta, from whom David Wardale acknowledges that he received much inspiration. No one denies the qualified success of the SAR class 26, but as yet no one has been able to determine the success (or otherwise) of No. 1816 because although limited trials have been carried out since the locomotive was transferred to Marcelo Salado from Unidad Proletaria Mill in 1996/7, no serious tests seem to have been made yet to decide whether Porta-isation is worth while or not.

But whatever the result, it has something else in common with the SAR class 26 besides its colour ... it is undeniably a very fine-looking machine indeed. It was originally a 1919 product of Alco's Schenectady Works; it has the Works No. 58751 and is one of a pair of American locomotives in Cuba on which L. D. Porta was reported to have carried out improvement experiments during the 1990s. The other one is No. 1750, a Baldwin 2-8-0 of 1925 (Works No. 58537) and is a José R. Riquelme locomotive, although not much has been heard lately about the progress on it.

No. 1816 spent two or three seasons at Marcelo Salado and the above photograph shows it at rest outside the shed there on Friday 5th March, 1999. However, visitors to Cuba for the 2000 *zafra* were delighted to discover that some real work had been found for it that year and it was at last seen to be earning its living hauling heavy cane trains on inter-mill workings from Eduardo García Lavandero, a mill to the west of Havana and one that does not normally see a great number of visiting enthusiasts. When news of No. 1816's involvement there spread amongst enthusiasts, E. G. Lavandero suddenly became an extremely popular mill indeed!

L. D. Porta must be very disappointed with the Cuban response to all his hard work because it seems that in the end, no more than just a little interest has ever been shown by the authorities and there is a noticeable lack of commitment to carry out any further experimentation. It would surely have been a boost to Cuba's international standing if it could have been said that they had modernised their ageing steam locomotive stock into the most efficient fleet in the world. Unfortunately, it seems that the whole idea was merely a pipe-dream and thus could well become something to be severely regretted in the not-too-distant future.

Mill 504, Ecuador - Standard Gauge

Of the four mills 'surrounding' Ciego de Ávila, Ecuador is the furthest away at some twenty five miles by road, although it is no more than fifteen as the crow flies. A giant cog-wheel beside the main Ciego - Holguín road indicates to car-drivers which turning to take for the mill, but if potential visitors realise that the mill-town is called Baraguá, that will help because there is a sign-post to that effect at the junction. Most mill-towns have the same name as the adjacent mill and Ecuador is unusual in that it differs from this norm. Rafael Freyre Mill is at Santa Lucìa and Boris Luis Santa Coloma is at Madruga, but all the other mills featured have mill-towns with the same name as the mills.

There are extensive sidings at Ecuador, as indeed there are at all four of Ciego's nearby mills and it was in those mill sidings that there was a quite serious collision between two locomotives in 1997. No. 1649 (Baldwin Mogul of 1919) was the yard shunter at the time and was between duties when it was struck quite forcefully by No. 1817 (Alco Consolidation of 1919) at the head of an incoming loaded cane train which resulted in both locomotives being severely damaged. As at Augusto César Sandino (see page 22), no one was injured too much, but apparently both crews were partly to blame as it seems that No. 1649 had been left fouling an incoming line and No. 1817

was travelling so fast along it that it was unable to stop when it was realised that there was a blockage. In the interests of producing the maximum amount of sugar each *zafra*, perhaps safety is not always uppermost in the minds of mill workers.

In the scene above, Baldwin 2-8-0 No. 1821 of 1920 (Works No. 52944) has just run right through the yard with a loaded train from the east and is about to come to rest before setting back onto a line that will allow entry to the mill for processing. It is not an uncommon sight to see at least three steam locomotives at work in this yard and, on most days in past seasons, there has been high activity here as dusk approaches. We can only hope that it will continue.

For many years, Ecuador's *jefe* was one Ethelbert Scantelbury, a tall and distinguished-looking ex-Trinidadian who personally welcomed enthusiasts to his sphere of influence, whether he knew them from previous visits or not. He spoke with a most endearing West Indian/English accent and has been sadly missed from the railway since his retirement in the late 1990s. He once mentioned that he ran the only cricket team in Cuba, but never explained who, if this was the case, formed his opposition! Visits to Ecuador have not been quite the same since Ethelbert decided to concentrate on playing dominoes instead of 'playing' with steam locomotives.

Mill 515, Ciro Redondo - Standard Gauge

Whether visitors stay in Ciego de Ávila or in Morón, Ciro Redondo Mill is no more than a thirty minute drive away and the system is such that it might well be that steam-hauled trains are encountered en route as mill lines cross main roads at more than one point. The system is probably the most extensive of all those in the country which are worked by steam and in past years the mill's yards were rarely to be seen without at least one Consolidation moving wagons. All operational locomotives at Ciro Redondo are large (and matching) 2-8-0s.

The level of working there has not changed substantially in recent times, but unfortunately the level of steam working has, due mainly to the difficulty in keeping the locomotive fleet operational. In common with everywhere else where steam is in use on the island, few locomotives at Ciro Redondo have currently seen less than eighty summers. This has necessitated the cannibalisation of some of the stock and caused the subsequent unwelcome (by many enthusiasts) influx of diesels. Diesels are used at most Cuban mills to a greater or lesser extent and the four which surround Ciego de Ávila have all been noted using them during the 1990s, but there are still sufficient steam locomotives available to do the bulk of the work throughout the area ... just.

Besides the influx of diesels, modernisation has reared its ugly head in other directions too and, as an example, the wonderfully ancient wooden signal-cabin cum family-residence

which guarded the flat crossing with the FCC south of the mill and which was partly shown on the left of the photograph on page 48 in Vol. One has now been demolished to make way for an extremely unattractive breeze-block structure on the same site. Steam trains always used to stop there for orders and, once these were received, drivers would feel able to set off across the FCC irrespective of whether the signal was 'on' or 'off', so one is left to speculate what purpose the semaphore actually serves. Telephone hand-sets are usually carried on Cuba's sugar locomotives anyway (no doubt they would not last long if left at the lineside!), so the reconstruction of the house by the crossing is even harder to comprehend.

The illustrations on these two pages show a pair of Ciro Redondo's 'identical' Consolidations hard at work in the mill yard. Above, No. 1828 (a Baldwin of 1920 with the Works No. 52970) is shown as it was on Thursday 27th February, 1997 setting back a loaded train across one of the many level crossings at the yard to the obvious inconvenience of the cyclists waiting below the tall semaphore signal on the left. No doubt there is a similar number of cyclists waiting on the right, hidden from view by the train, yet impatience is rarely shown in these circumstances; it's just an everyday fact of life in a Cuban mill town. No. 1829 has always been at Ciro Redondo and was originally the Cuba Cane Sugar Company's No. 101.

Opposite, Baldwin 2-8-0 No. 1832 of 1920 (Works No. 53952) was caught on film (again

delaying a cyclist) as it too was labouring hard in the mill yard on Friday 24th March, 1995. To all intents and purposes 'twin' locomotives, Nos. 1828 and 1832 do have one noticeable difference as the observant reader will have spotted already. The former machine still sports what must be its original lipped chimney whilst the latter, like most of Ciro Redondo's working engines, has been given one of the much less attractive stove-pipes; a change obviously forced by necessity. Together (irrespective of chimney) they constitute as fine a sight as any of the fleets of large locomotives on the island. Yes, the men in Cuba's engine sheds really earn their meagre pay with the way they maintain (most of) their charges in such grand condition and in 2000 had even managed to turn out one locomotive (No. 1827) in green! Well done indeed.

How to survive a whole day out in a hire car in Cuba is something which one learns from experience and experience dictates that taking a vacuum flask with an ice-cold drink in it is a good way to start the day, but the heat of the Caribbean often means that by lunch-time all the drink has been consumed, so alternatives have to be sought. At Ciro Redondo, a tried and tested alternative is to knock on (almost) any door and ask for cold water; a plea which the author has never had refused. Water in Cuba is guaranteed pure and tastes delicious. Away from the big cities there are no added chemicals (at least, none that can be tasted) and much of the supply comes straight out of deep wells. Whether or not it has any therapeutic value is not known, but on taste alone, it is very highly recommended.

During a recent visit to Ciro Redondo, the author needed his flask replenishing and, acting on his own advice, knocked on the door of a house beside the yard to beg for water for himself and some of his group. A nice, young, English-speaking lady (who turned out to be the mill dentist on her day off) answered and insisted that she and her family make a 'special' drink for the visitors and wouldn't take "No" for an answer. Wondering what on earth would follow, the group was led into the garden where there was a lime tree absolutely bursting with fruit and below it a sort of Heath Robinson mangle machine that was used to extract liquid sugar direct from cane.

The delicious taste of freshly crushed lime mixed with freshly crushed sugar cane plus ice-cubes is something which is not easily forgotten and had it not been for the need to photograph the steam locomotives hard at work outside, much more 'nectar' might well have been consumed than was strictly necessary that particular afternoon. Payment in any form was politely but firmly refused, of course, and it would have been oh so easy to take advantage of these incredibly poor but hospitable people, yet their actions were typical of the vast majority of Cubans who, irrespective of the steam, make a visit to the island such a pleasant and unforgettable experience.

Mill 503, Orlando González Ramirez - Standard Gauge

As outlined on page 43 in the earlier book, O. G. R.'s lines go both north and south out of the mill and although the steam-worked section of the line to the north is only a mile or so long, the southern sections go very much further. So much further in fact that one of them eventually makes a connection with Venezuela Mill way over to the east. It is the line which eventually swings round to the west that attracts most enthusiasts though, as it is at the far end that the highly prized photographs of street running in Limones Palmero might be obtained.

What has not been mentioned previously however, is that there is a short branch off this line which travels mainly northwards through the tiny hamlet of Las Trozas to an *acopio* just past it and the photograph on this page (taken on Easter Monday, 8th April, 1996) is of a short train as it was leaving there to rejoin the loaded wagons from Limones which it had temporarily abandoned on the main line some thirty minutes earlier. The little branch generally does not see too much use and two reasons have been put forward for this. Firstly, it has been suggested that the *acopio* would appear to have a poor record of reliability and secondly, the water-capacity of some locomotives' tenders is insufficient to cater for the extra time involved for the diversion, short though it may be.

No. 1836 (2-8-0 Vulcan of 1922, Works No. 3148) was the locomotive in use along the branch that Easter weekend and, as can be seen from the leaves on the palm trees, there was a full gale blowing at the time. Windy conditions can often be very tricky for photographers because exhaust smoke can be blown down to obliterate parts of the locomotive and the train from view, not to mention the fact that it can cause other awkward shadows, but here the breeze was being blown in the photographers' favour, for which they were all extremely grateful.

Originally allocated to Panamá Mill in Camagüey Province where it ran as No. 2, No. 1836 was for a while at Primero de Enero Mill which, like O. G. R., is in Ciego de Ávila Province. Locomotives have always moved about between mills in Cuba and one of the joys of a yearly visit is to discover what changes have taken place since the previous *zafra*. Keeping up with these changes is of great interest, of course and it should always be born in mind that locomotive allocations are not etched in stone so that, subject to gauge, almost any locomotive could turn up almost anywhere on the island. Fortunately, the influx of diesels has not been as swift or as penetrating as was feared, but it is happening, albeit slowly, so it would be very unwise to expect any particular locomotive to be at any particular mill for certain. These things can change, and sometimes they do, even today.

Mill 318, Victoria de Yaguajay - Standard Gauge

We have seen on pages 16 and 26 how Simón Bolivar and Obdulio Morales Mills are situated only a mile or so apart and 'share' each others' locomotives, but they are not the only 'twin' mills in Cuba where this has happened. Granma and Victoria de Yaguajay Mills are even closer than the other two and, until the mid 1990s, it was usual for both mills to turn out locomotives as required, but V. de Yaguajay always seemed to be the one which was closed. It has not seen use for some years now and, whilst it is always dangerous to say that any mill has been closed permanently, it certainly looks as if that is so there. Thus in the case illustrated on this page, it was to Granma that cane from the area went for processing and up to 2000, it did still.

Granma Mill will always have a special place in the author's affections because not only was it the first Cuban sugar mill he ever visited, it contained the first Cuban steam locomotives he ever saw and it was also the first place in Cuba where he was invited up onto a footplate for a ride, including a drive. Momentous happenings like that are not easily forgotten.

Photographed on Tuesday 8th March, 1994 as it shunted near V. de Yaguajay's mill, No. 1813 is that most popular combination amongst Cuba's steam locomotives, a 1920-built 2-8-0 by Baldwin and it has the Works No. 54138. After marshalling a length of empties that morning, No. 1813 ran smoke-box forward to the nearby town of Coliseo where it ran round and then set off, tender first, on MINAZ track which parallels the FCC south-eastwards from here for about ten miles. The big Consolidation dropped off wagons at various *acopios* along the way until it reached journey's end near Jovellanos and returned along the same route with an ever lengthening train of loaded wagons, ultimately to be delivered to Granma.

Mill 440, Ifraín Alfonso - Standard Gauge

The two biggest working steam locomotives in Cuba are allocated to Ifraín Alfonso, a mill situated close to the *autopista* just off the 'Road to the Mills'. Both engines are younger than almost any other on the island, both are 2-8-2s and both arrived at Ifraín during the early 1990s, although they came from different mills at different times. They were described and illustrated in Vol. One (on pp 37/38), but it is thought that because of their importance within the overall steam scene, it is only right and proper that they should be shown again now, especially since the views this time are completely different from the earlier ones.

No. 1850, shown in silhouette above, is a Baldwin of 1935 (Works No. 61888) and No. 1910 (opposite) was constructed in the Brooks Works of Alco in 1925 with the Works No. 66284. On arrival, they joined a 2-6-2, a 2-8-0 and a 4-6-0 (shown on pp 34-36 of Volume One) which were already at Ifraín, thus giving the mill's five main line locomotives four different wheel arrangements, something not seen anywhere else in Cuba. All five have been in use during the 1990s.

The silhouette photograph was taken on Sunday 13th March, 1994 and shows No. 1850 at the start of the final climb towards the mill with apparently no one on the footplate,

perhaps being driven by remote control by the gentleman sitting at the back end of the tender. Or perhaps not! Working patterns on mill railways change continuously as they are mainly dependent upon the availability of the cut cane out in the fields and during much of the 1994 *zafra,* a train would return to the mill round about dusk to the great delight of waiting photographers.

To get the 'right' angle for the photograph with the setting sun in the 'right' place between the trees meant standing beside a rat-infested open sewer, but fortunately our furry friends were not interested in humans on this occasion, even though the photographers were more than interested in the rats! Nevertheless, as soon as the shot was in the bag, there was definitely no reason to hang about and a swift exit was made through a conveniently positioned under-pass, unsurprisingly with all haste possible.

One reason why such large locomotives are in use at Ifraín Alfonso is that the line is quite steeply graded in places and another is that trains here are often quite heavy. Put those two things together and fireworks can follow, literally. Just off to the left of the photograph of No. 1910 crossing the Great Cuban Highway, the line starts to climb sharply, but on Wednesday 4th April, 1996 it was all a bit too much for the big locomotive and its

long, loaded train because at the first attempt it got nowhere near the summit and had to set back in disgrace across the road for another run at the gradient. The same thing happened at the second attempt too, so back it all went again only then it went a lot further. The photograph is actually of the third (that time, successful) attempt at the incline and the small group of on-lookers by the bridge could hardly believe their luck. They had seen five crossings of the *autopista* in no more than about twenty minutes. What a morning!

All road vehicles are required by Cuban law to stop at level crossings, so they are natural spots for roadside entrepreneurs to congregate. The person wearing the grass hat in the central reservation of the motorway (standing just below the cab of the locomotive) is not trying to thumb a lift, as it appears, but is in reality a garlic-vendor. As such, he is obviously someone from whom it is definitely prudent to keep a respectable distance, odour-wise, which may be why, in this photograph, he is alone. However, Cuban road users in general have a totally relaxed attitude to highway regulations, so by no means all drivers even slow down, let alone stop, but those who do are subjected to much garlic-waving as the would-be sellers do their utmost to unload their wares onto the passing population. How any sort of living is made at this is a mystery because no matter how hard they try, they never ever seem to be able to sell anything.

In 1998 the mill was not in operation, but some of its locomotives were and generally they worked on inter-mill journeys to various mills in the vicinity which gave interesting sights of steam travelling along FCC lines, something not seen with any degree of regularity. Trains leaving Ifraín Alfonso Mill normally take the left-hand line at the junction with the FCC and go left again shortly afterwards in order to head back north across the Great Cuban Highway on their way to Pozo at the far end of the line, but when Ifraín cannot cope with the cane, it is not unusual for trains to keep straight on at this point towards mills such as Diez de Octubre as happened in 1997 when Ifraín's 4-6-0 No.1636 was spotted there beside the huge portrait of Che Guevara.

It is also possible for trains to take the right-hand road after leaving the mill and go through the old station of Santa María (the pre-revolution name of Ifraín Alfonso) to reach mills such as Carlos Caraballo and Marta Abreu and in 1999 there was also inter-mill working with steam between these last two, which involved running through the picturesque town of Cruces. Much of this FCC running goes unseen by enthusiasts, of course, because unless they happen to be at the right place at the right time, the chances are that they won't know anything about it until it's too late.

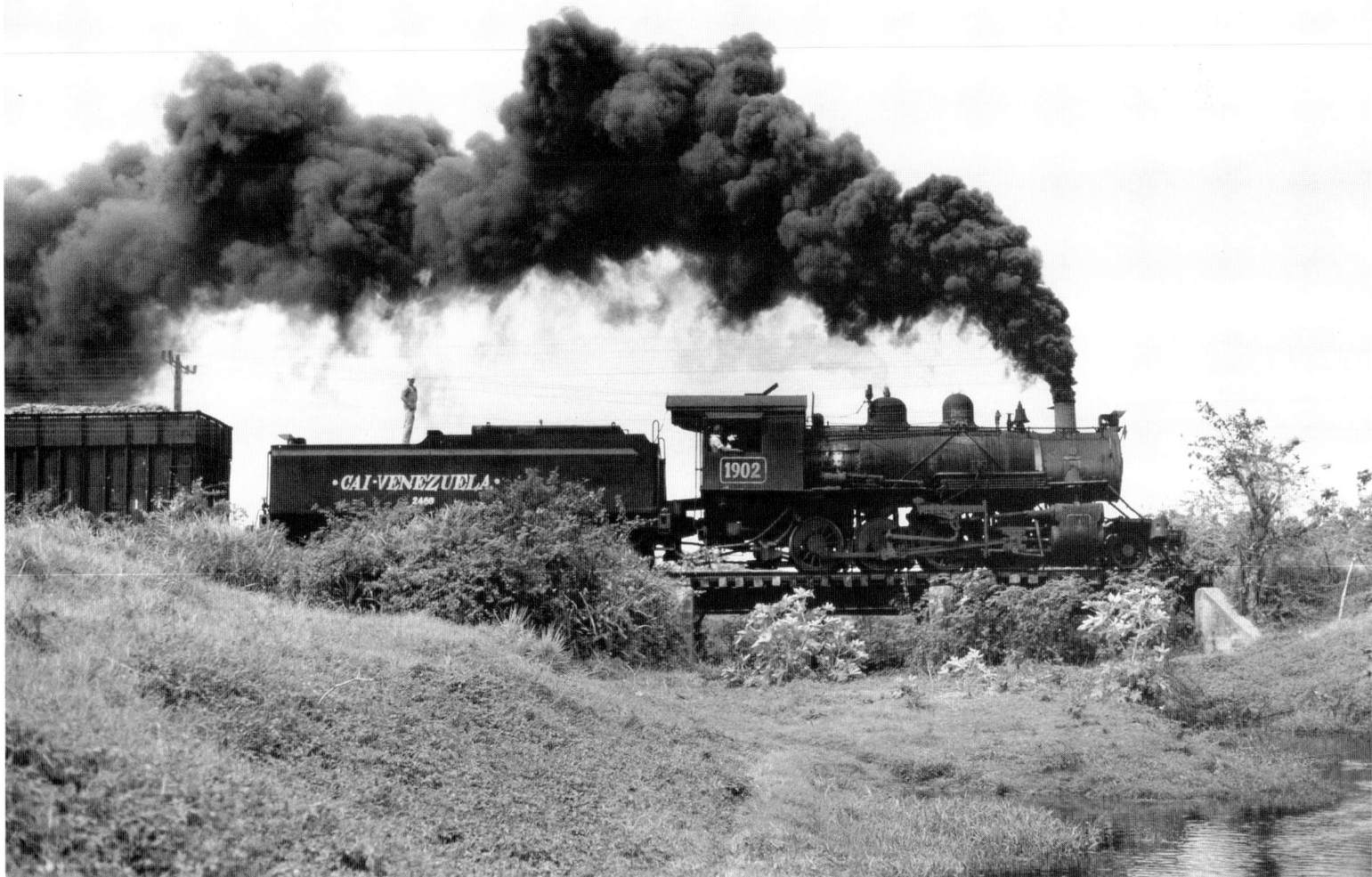

Mill 522, Venezuela - Standard Gauge

The Venezuela system is generally regarded as being one of two parts (the east line and the west line) and on leaving the mill to the south (which all trains out into the fields must do), those for the east line (eventually to run past 'The Tree', see page 39) branch off in that direction immediately. Trains of empties for the western part of the system continue south for about a mile before swinging to the right and then generally heading in a westerly direction until the furthest *acopio* from the mill is reached. The photograph on this page was taken at the exact point where that line starts to swing right, although what is depicted is in fact a loaded train returning to the mill one morning. The date was Thursday 5th March, 1998.

A dirt road parallels the railway along there which considerably eases access to the line for photographic purposes, although bushes growing close to the track can present a bit of a problem. Consequently this little bridge is quite a popular spot amongst photographers as it gives an unimpeded view of the locomotive and allows some of the 'brook' to be included in the scene. However, the brook is far from being the idyllic little stream that it appears and woe betide anybody who is unfortunate enough to put any part of his body in it because it consists of what is probably as lethal a cocktail of oil, effluent and mill waste-products as there is in the whole of Cuba. Nose-pegs are a distinct advantage anywhere near this fast-flowing but deadly stretch of 'water'.

No. 1902 has all the appearance of being a sheep in wolf's clothing, or lamb dressed as mutton if you prefer because although it can clearly be seen to be carrying a 19xx number, it looks to be no bigger than any 18xx locomotive and about the same size as most 17xx. But 19xx it is and it is the only one of this classification at Venezuela. Built by the Vulcan Iron Works at Wilkes-Barre in 1920, the 2-8-0 has the Works No. 3004 and has spent almost all its life at this mill. When constructed it was to fill an order from the Cuba Northern Railroad and was to have been their No. 45, but Venezuela Mill (then known as Stewart) became its home instead. It did find gainful employment at Primero de Enero for a while, but that mill has been defunct for many a long day now and No. 1902 has not wandered away from Venezuela since its return.